WHAT'S IN A NAME ?
HISTORY AND MEANING OF WYCKOFF

By M. William Wykoff

Rochester, N.Y.   2014

CreateSpace Independent Publishing Platform
ISBN-10: 1500379956
ISBN-13: 978-1500379957

M. William Wykoff
236 Trafalgar Street
Rochester, N.Y. 14619
mwwykoff@gmail.com

Cover: Ansicht auf Marienhafe um 1400, oil painting by Gerhard H. Janssen. For a description and the significance of the cover, go to page 23.

Dedications

To Wilhelm J. Wykhoff of Scharnebeck, Lower Saxony, and the late Hans Schrader of Smithtown, Long Island, authors of the article published in the 1988 Wyckoff family *Bulletin* that inspired me to launch further investigations into the origin of our American progenitor.

To the volunteer genealogists and historians who assembled the lineages for three editions of *The Wyckoff Family of America* and have helped many a potential member of the Wyckoff Association of America establish eligibility to grow a limb on the Wykoff family tree. I can recall only some who answered queries over the years: Daisy Rathbun, John L. Ely, Helen Wikoff, Eleanore White, and Margaret Moore.

To the late Frans van Coetsam of Cornell University, a most enthusiastic, knowledgeable gentleman, scholar of Germanic linguistics, and a wonderful mentor who encouraged me to persist in my quest for the truth about my ancestor.

Acknowledgements

The local historian of Marienhafe, Harm Bents, answered my every query in record time. His meticulous attention to detail made him the ideal proofreader for this printed edition. If any typos or misspellings in English or German remain, they are solely the responsibility of the author. This booklet has benefitted immeasurably from the knowledge and intelligence of Harm Bents. The diligent genealogist and beekeeper, Kay Blass, born in Wittmund, East Frisia, now living in Berlin, first brought my attention to the potential significance of the emblem scripted by Pieter Claessen. It was she who sent me a copy of the 1622 *Viehschatzung* (census of cattle owners) for the area including Marienhafe. She certainly went out of her way, making every effort to provide me with information and copies of pertinent documents. The competent genealogists extraordinaire, Perry Streeter, Renee Dauven, Bryce Stevens, and Stephan Clarke contributed genuine acts of encouragement for which I am truly grateful.

Introduction

The Wyckoff surname has a specific origin but many Wyckoff family members in America believe mistakenly the name to be Dutch. Wyckoff is actually a Frisian name which indicates the settlement from where the first male progenitor of the Wyckoff family in America originated. Names very similar to Wyckoff are found in several coastal areas all around the North Sea and the Western Baltic, where the Germanic name translates as a settlement on a bay. It stems from the same Indo-Germanic root *wik as found in the word *Viking,* and from a much earlier Proto Indo-European word root *weik, as reflected in Greek, *woikos* or *oikos,* referring to a household. Latin *vicus* refers to a living area, specifically a quarter or district of a larger settlement. In the Brookmerland area of East Frisia whence Pieter Claessen emigrated to New Netherland, the meaning of the Northern German word root may have taken on specific local connotations which need to be considered carefully and critically. The current popularized (but false) meaning of the surname was fabricated in America by a well-intentioned Wyckoff family genealogist. The popularized history of the European origins of Pieter Claessen stems from a sordid account authored by one fraudulent Gustave Anjou. Not all Wyckoffs in America descend from Pieter Claessen. Other Wyckoff immigrants who came from Germany later often spelled the name slightly differently. The Wyckoff name is not unique to America. In current European telephone books, it occurs principally in the Lower Saxony area of northern Germany.

History

The focus here is on the history of the surname as the title implies, not on the history of the immigrant, Pieter Claessen, and his American descendants. The facts about the ethnic and geographical origins of Pieter Claessen have been known for decades, even in the absence of direct genealogical evidence. Unfortunately, the facts have been imperspicuously interwoven with fictive genealogy and etymology. The additional, historical facts presented here on the surname are demonstrative and serve to further separate the wheat from the fictive extraneous chaff. By focussing on the family name rather than on the person, it is possible to lend further credence to what is already known about the origins of Pieter Claessen. The audience I anticipate for this treatise includes tens of thousands who have some ancestral connection to *Wykhoff* (in all of its various spellings) not just in America but also in Germany. In fact, in writing this essay, most of my sources are German, and much productive assistance has come from Harm Bents, the local historian in Marienhafe, and from Kay Blaas, a genealogist born in Wittmund, Ostfriesland; (East Frisia) now living in Berlin. The numerous Wykhoff families in Germany today did not descend from Pieter Claessen. What they share with Wykhoffs everywhere is their Frisian place of origin. If any Wyckoffs are ever discovered and documented in Holland, their ancestors are most likely to have originated in Friesland.

There are countless Americans and people of all nationalities seeking to discover the meaning of their surname on dozens of websites; some purport to offer general databases on names; others are dedicated to names grouped by language or nationality. Most genealogical websites have at least a brief paragraph devoted to the meaning of each family name. Unfortunately, the inquisitive seeker often finds only hearsay (often contradictory) or false information repeated on these websites. Even in standard, printed dictionaries such as the 3-volume Oxford *Dictionary of American Family Names,* 2002), incomplete information and even errors are commonly presented. A tremendous amount of work remains to be accomplished regarding the place of origin and earlier meanings of surnames, but I submit here that we have made some genuine progress in determining the meaning of *Wykhof* in actual speech communities over time and space.

American genealogists and historians are typically narrowly focussed. Without linguistic training they regard etymology and philology as esoteric fields, peripheral to their task, and problematic as historical methodology. If the reader is willing to follow this adventure into the unfamiliar territory of historical linguistics, he or she will discover not only that the ancestral surname was definitely not Dutch, but will be led to much more illuminating factual information. While linguistic methodology cannot span intercontinental migrations of homonids over millions of years which DNA methodology does very well, linguistics can, through reconstruction, take us back far enough to the Indo Germanic language of the pre-agricultural neolithic pastoralists, and to analyses of later North Germanic as transcribed in late medieval documents shedding much light on the Wykhof household south of Norden, first constructed around AD1250. Facts revealed by historical linguistics and dialect geography are quite pertinent to the meaning and location of The Wykhof. We may never know the history of Pieter

Claessen's youth. We may never know the identity of his parents (genealogy). But a philological study of his surname including the generic meaning of a settlement on a bay, and local meaningful adaptations to environmental hydrology, climate change, maritime trading, place of refuge for pirates, epidemiology, Christianity, and Zeitgeist, are all revealing and relative to the youthful existence of Pieter Claessen at the place of his birth. One cannot hope to explain a new connotation or meaning attached to a surname unless one understands the cultural and environmental context of the speech community in which the change occurred.

Extensive data on descendants of Pieter Wyckoff, many of whom settled in New Jersey in the 18th century,[1] have been verified provisionally, and arranged in great detail in *Wyckoff Family in America,* published in 1950.[2] After several updates, the most recent edition can be ordered as a CD from the website: www.wyckoffassociation.org. Much current information about the Wyckoff Farm House Museum in Brooklyn is disseminated at the same website. The facts about the life of Pieter Wyckoff in the New Netherland colony are well known from the extensive documentation of colonial administrators.[3] However, the origins of the surname and of the man himself as formerly disseminated by the Wyckoff Association of America, and often repeated on genealogy websites and even in genealogy journals are simply wrong. Unfortunately, the critical sources cited, although they employ voluminous documentation, are ultimately creative works of fiction.

---

[1] Within a few generations, there were more Wyckoff families in Bergen, Somerset, Hunterdon, Monmouth, and Middlesex Counties in New Jersey than in all of New York. See various county histories such as: *History of Hunterdon and Somerset Counties, New Jersey with Illustrations and Biographical Sketches of the Prominent Men and Pioneers.* Compiled by James P. Snell. Philadelphia: Everts & Peck, 1881. Although many of these pioneers became prominent businessmen, their more humble origins including the illegitimcy of some of their ancestors are often forgotten, ignored, or unknown.

[2] Wyckoff Association in America, *The Wyckoff Family in America, A Genealogy.* (Rutland, Vermont: Tuttle Publishing Company, Inc. 1950). An earlier (1934) and now rare version of *The Wyckoff Family in America: A Genealogy* (Rutland, Vermont) was edited by Mr. and Mrs. Milford B. Streeter. For additional information on sources, see section below, Notes on Wyckoff Documentary History, p. 47.

[3] "The Rise of Pieter Claessen Wyckoff: Social Mobility on the Colonial Frontier,"*New York History* 53.1 (January 1972): 4-24, by Morton Wagmann serves as a brief biography of our immigrant ancestor.

Although there were Wykhoffs who emigrated from Germany after the 17th century, the majority of people in America named Wyckoff descend from one early settler, a young laborer, probably an orphan in his late teens who arrived in 1637. Pieter Claessen had no surname until coerced by the English conquerors of New Amsterdam to adopt one in 1687, fifty years after his arrival in America. Before Pieter adopted the surname Wyckoff, he, like many of his illiterate immigrant neighbors and acquaintances, signed documents with an *X* which required the presence and signature of a responsible literate witness. On the 10th of July, 1655, Pieter Claesen entered into a contract negotiated by Cornelis van Tienhoven on behalf of the Director General of the Dutch West Indies Company, Petrus Stuyvesant, to superintend his bowery and cattle at Amesfoort (Brooklyn). The *X* was witnessed by Secretary Cornelis Ruyven.[4] On another occasion, Pieter Claessen made an emblematic sign (see facsimile below) that has been interpreted as an anchor, but, as pointed out by Kay Blaas (pers. comm.), the sign resembles a Hausmarke, a unique hand drawn sign for a family residence that was still used by illiterate persons, of whom there were many during the early 1600s in Friesland. (From time immemorial, neither the

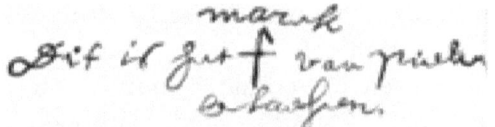

alphabet nor Arabic numerals were taught in northern Europe. Arabic numbers were not adopted by Europeans until during the early Renaissance). Houses were not numbered, but instead were identified by unique black and white line drawings. Eventually, the Hausmarke fell into disuse. Households came to be identified by surnames or surname monograms, and were numbered. In 1856, The Wykhoff was Haus Nr. 126.

---

⁴ O'Callaghan, E.B. (ed.), *Documents Relating to the Colonial History of the State of New York, Procured in Holland, England, and France by John Romeyn Brodhead, XIV: 328* (Albany: Weed, Parsons and Company. 1853-87). Other examples of the sign can be found in: *Town Records of Kings County. Flatlands Deeds, Town Orders, Road Records-1674-1828. Miscellaneous Papers-1661-1831. Municipal Archives of the City of New York, NY. Town Records Series Microfilm No. 75, item 4000 (includes item 4006), Flatlands Miscellaneous Records (Indian Deeds, Petitions, Awards, Court Records, Quitrent Receipts) 1661-1864)* p. 52]. Sources provided by Renee L. Dauven (pers. comm. 2/28/14).

In a typewritten list of Hausmarken from the *Marienhafer Armenprotokollbuche,* assembled from the original handwritten *Armen-Legaten-Buch,* only one Hausmarke similar to that used by Pieter Claessen is to be found, in a 1657 entry. (It appears as #43 on the modern type-scripted list. Only a vertical line to form a plus (+) is adjoined on the left side of the sign made by Pieter Claessen. As pointed out by Harm Bents (pers.comm.), the sign is taken from page 107 of the original handwritten Marienhafe *Armen-Legaten-Buch* which contains records pertaining to the poor from 1619 to 1749. The volume is archived in the Kirchengemeinde Marienhafe.

```
43.×Poptet Ehmen marck   -|^
```

Because of the individual uniqueness of these signs, one can infer a possible relationship between this later sign with that familiar to Pieter Claessen who left Marienhafe many years earlier. In keeping with the charity practices of the church established by Martin Luther, several elders of Marienkirche signed their names to verify the annual (Feb.1655--Feb.1656) expenses for the poor, elderly, orphans, widows, and the sick or disabled. Among the church elders listed were Ehme Poptes and Poptet Ehmen, whom Kay Blaas (pers comm.) interprets as father and son. Traditionally, only the eldest son could utilize the original Hausmarke. Younger illiterate sons were obliged to use a modified version (Harm Bents, pers. comm). Proof is unlikely to be forthcoming, but one can surmise that this generic Hausmarke without the plus (+) may have been the mark associated with Pieter Claessen's guardian or godfather. It is then possible that the church elder, Ehme Poptes, knew the mother of Pieter, the local Pastor Nicolaus, and could have been present at the baptism of Pieter Claessen. But a similarity of signs is insufficient evidence to establish a specific relationship. Without further documentation, this interpretation must remain hypothetical.

As an orphan in America, it is difficult to imagine what, if any, authority Pieter Claessen invoked by utilizing the sign, but for the illiterate in Ostfrisland, it was customary for contracts to be signed utilizing the Hausmarke. Clearly, Pieter was using a family emblem long before he had to adopt a surname. Pieter Claessen did not know how to spell his name but he knew where he came from and he knew the name by which it was called. It is significant that he chose Wyckoff, not Norden, even though the Norden township border could have encircled The Wykhof in the 1630s. When he and his sons were finally required to adopt a surname and he swore his allegiance to the British ruler, it should not be surprising that Wyckoff was spelled the local way in New Amsterdam and signed by Garret Strijcker (but printed as Strycker) who was Sheriff of Kings County, the local area of the Dutch-speaking community in which they were living. In Ostfriesland (East Frisia), when persons from Wykhof were finally required to take a surname in 1811, they consistently retained the h- in hoff. Variations in the spelling of the surname in English, Frisian, German, and American Dutch include Wykoff, Wykhoff, Wykhof, Wyckoff, Wijckoff, Wycoff, Wicoff, Wikoff, Wieckhof, Wickhoff, Waychoff, Wechhof, Weckauf, et al. Generally, spellings with -hof (as in Wykhof, Wykhoff, Wiekhoff, and Wickhof) are Frisian and German; spellings with -ij- are Dutch; spellings with -y- are English. Occasionally, early scribes in New Netherland used the Frisian spelling rather than the Dutch or English, but it is not known if this signified a conscious awareness that our progenitor spoke Frisian. There is more spelling variation within English than in the other languages. The particular variation cited in documents should be cited wherever possible. As an example, it was properly recorded in New York on 5 August 1727 that Sara Dirckse married Pieter Wycoff, and the witnesses were Claes Wykhof and Willemtje Wykof.[5] If all the many variants were listed only under a single standard, it would only lead to conflation and confusion. The differences are sometimes highly significant for genealogical sleuthing. Herein, I employ the variant as given in the source being referred to, or paraphrased, but in my own discourse I attempt to be consistent by employing only one form for a person or place name, such as Pieter Claessen or Marienhafe, in the many temporal and spatial contexts of my narrative.

In the European tradition, the first-born male was usually given the first name of his paternal grandfather. The second born male was given the name of his maternal grandfather. Pieter Claessen (or Niclaesen), who finally adopted Wyckoff as his patronym, was probably the son of one Claus (or Niclaus or Nicolaus). Because we don't know whether Pieter had older male siblings, we cannot know whether Pieter was actually named after his paternal, or maternal, grandfather, or some other relative. Pieter Claessen bestowed the name Nicholas (nickname Claes, or Claus) on his first son born in America. Undoubtedly in accord with his wife Grietje, he named his second son, Cornelis, after his father-in-law, Cornelis van Ness. Thus, in accord with tradition, each of his first two sons was respectively named after his paternal and maternal

---

[5] *The New York Genealogical and Biographical Record* 64.4 (1933): 372.

grandfather. The names of his daughters Margrietje, Maycke, and Annetje occur in the family of his wife. We may speculate then that Willemptje and Geertje may have been taken from his side of the family.

In the coastal lowlands surrounding the North Sea, the names Pieter Claessen and Claes Pietersson were ubiquitous, and birth records with surnames of parents were normally non-existent except for the nobility. Thus, genealogists have to be especially circumspect before linking the American Pieter Claessen with any combination of these two popular names found in European documents. Even if an actual birth or baptismal certificate of a Pieter Claessen were to be found that can be associated with a son of a well-to-do Dutch seaman named Claes Cornelisze, the fact that it vaguely coincides with the estimated birth year of our ancestor is no justification for establishing a genealogical link as was done by Gustave Anjou.[6] Pieter Claessen was most probably born several years before 1625. There is no sound reason to doubt that Pieter Claessen had his origins in the vicinity of Norden, Ostfriesland (East Frisia). It goes without saying that it is likely to be futile to search for the surname of Pieter Claessen in European documents. Until the eighteenth century, the majority of the population had no surnames. Before 1811, Frisian surnames were customarily utilized only by literate persons and owners of manorial estates. Pieter Claessen was von Norden (from the area of Norden) but he was no Van Norden. Very few from the elite classes ever settled in the American colonies.[7] The larger proportion of emigrants to New Netherland were from the lower classes and had little chance for advancement in rigidly stratified

---

[6] Documents are too easily created. A document cannot be considered absolute as it often is in genealogy. As DNA paternity tests have shown, judges and jurists are not even obliged to believe the testimony of the mother. Historians have learned to consider the preponderance of evidence. Even circumstantial evidence is to be preferred over a document if the evidence is consistent, connected, and conclusive. And church records of baptisms and deaths did not often survive more than a few generations even when they were not destroyed by fires and floods.

[7] J. Gardner Bartlett, the genealogical authority on New England remarked, "Of the five thousand heads of families who came between 1620 and 1640, less than 50 or not 1% are known to have belonged to the upper gentry of England, and less than 250 more, or not 5% can be considered as from the minor mercantile or landed gentry." Quoted in *Genealogical Evidence, A Guide to the Standard of Proof Relating to Pedigrees, Ancestry, Heirship and Family History* by Noel C. Stevenson. (Aegean Park Press, rev. ed., 1989): 30.

European societies. They stemmed from an ancient feudal system, and suffered from lack of education, restricted mobility, and severe marriage restrictions. Most listed their occupations as farm laborers, soldiers, or craftsmen and many of them were non-Dutch. Of the soldiers hired by the West India Company to fight Indians and protect the colony from the English and other European colonizers, 68% came from countries outside the Dutch Republic. The majority were from German provinces and many decided to stay in New Netherland and take up another trade at the expiration of their contract.[8]

Very few immigrants were middle-class Dutch burghers of the ruling, regents class.[9] Pieter was an illiterate laborer. His mother could have been attached to the Wykhof in Brookmerland in sundry servant capacities. There were special sleeping cupboards for the help. It is worth mentioning that there was a severe plague in 1635 claiming 236 lives within the small area of Kirchspiel Marienhafe which decimated the population.[10] It is a wonder that Pieter Claessen survived, and it is entirely possible that he was already an orphan or the illegitimate son of a female servant. (Illegitimacy was very common throughout Europe at the time and there was no great stigma attached to the status). What Pieter had in common with other Wykhofs from Marienhafe south of Norden, for certain, was their place of origin, not necessarily any genetic or familial relationship with the proprietor of the estate.[11] In fact, the

---

[8]   Jaap Jacobs, *The Colony of New Netherland: A Dutch Settlement in Seventeenth-Century America.* Ithaca, N.Y.: Cornell University Press. (2009): 38-39, citing F.S Gaastra, *De geschiedenis van de VOC (Zutphen 1991)*

[9]   David S. Cohen, "How Dutch Were the Dutch of New Netherland?" *New York History* 62 (1981):47.   Literate relatives of patroons were often given administrative positions in the colony but most returned eventually to the homeland. Of course, there were some notable exceptions.

[10]   Wilhelm J Wykhoff, *Die Geschichte der Familie Wykhoff,* (Vorwort). Scharnebeck: Selbstverlag, 2008. (A paperbound notebook with clippings, maps, genealogy lists, and pictures.)

[11]   In America, we can identify descendants of Pieter Claessen, and a DNA profile for the lineage is possible. According to information on the FindTheData website, about 8% of Wyckoffs in America are black, and it would not be surprising to find that many of them share the same genetic heritage as their white cousins. In Europe, we do not know the parentage of Pieter Claessen or whether he had any siblings. Thanks to the founder of the Wykhoff Association of Germany, Wilhelm J. Wykhoff, there are now reunions of families with the surname Wykhoff whose participants could be DNA tested, and compared to results of American descendants of Pieter Claessen. However, neither the German Wykhoffs nor the American Wyckoffs

builder of the first Wykhof house-barn south of Norden was most likely
Ast von Upgant. We do not yet know who occupied the house in the
year of Pieter Claessen's emigration, but records show that Hans
Harmens was the tenant in 1638. In the following decades the house
was then occupied by a family headed by a young man named Claess
Gauckes. The children of Gauckes were all named Klaessen or Klaasen
but all their births came long after the departure of Pieter Claessen.[12]
The bottom line that can be read (so far) from the fragmentary evidence
on successive owners and tenants of The Wykhof near Marienhafe over
several centuries is that none of them went by the name Wykhof.
Wykhof was a descriptive term for the residence. When the head of a
European household was required to adopt a family name, it was
customary to identify himself by his place of origin. Pieter Claessen
simply continued that tradition in America. When surnames gradually
became customary in Ostfriesland around 1769, the tenant at that time,
Casjen Janssen, adopted the surname, Wiekhoff. While the adoption of
a surname in New Netherland was mandated at the particular time of
the British takeover, surnames in Europe were adopted at different
times over decades according to provincial edicts and family
circumstances. As early as 1593, one Johan von Wikehof was employed
as a legal clerk in Aurich, so Pieter Claessen was not the first to identify
himself with another spelling version of Wykhof as his place of origin.[13]

As a footnote to the problem of Pieter Claessen's family origins
and the search for an adult Claes in Marienhafe, Kay Blaas recently (18
Feb 2014) sent me a copy of a local Marienhafe and Upgant census of
cattle owners and heads of households (Viehschatzung) dated 1622. She
had concluded that Claes, the father of Pieter Claessen was already
deceased by this time and that Pieter was probably an orphan or an

---

had surnames which can be traced back much earlier than 1600 which makes
any interpretation of results somewhat problematical.

[12] Harm Bents recently (2013) forwarded to me information from local
family histories, church books, and censuses that record the name Gauckes as
the occupant in records spanning 1663-1684. In archival records from Aurich,
compiled by Theodor Voss, a cryptic entry from 1632 reads "Uff Ilenßwerff -
.. Hanß in de Wyckhoff."

[13] Wiard Hinrichs, in a recent (March 2014) email to Kay Blaas, cites a
1593/94 census for the districts of Aurich, Friedeburg, Herrlichkeiten Gödens
and Kniphausen in which Johan von Wikehoff (Nr. 384) is listed as a legal
courier. We do not know the origin of Johan's family. It is worth noting that
there was a medieval Wik/Markt in the early history of Aurich (ca. AD 1250).

illegitimate youth. However, I noticed that a Pastor Nicolaus was among those listed. The Pastorenhaus (parsonage) frequently had one or more milk cows associated with it. One can only wonder if a milkmaid was hired. I suggested the possibility that Nicolaus could have fathered a child in Marienhafe. Pieter Claessen could have been an illegitimate Priesterkind of which there have been very many recorded throughout the history of the church. (Of course, no one knows how many went unrecorded). If this inference happens to be correct, then the father of Pieter was in the vicinity of Marienhafe and The Wykhoff only briefly. In a review of pastor successions in Marienhafe, the author of *Ostfriesländisches Prediger-Denkmahl* (Aurich 1796)[14] stated that Nicolaus Wennicerus (a given Latin surname) had been a Rektor in Aurich, came to Marienhafe in 1616, and died in 1622. Kay Blaas has confirmed that he was matriculated as Nicolaus Wennicerus in the University of Rostock in 1606/7. (Universität Rostock, founded in 1419, is the oldest university in Northern Europe, which was assigned the duty by Pope Martin V to drive off the northern darkness with the light of the Christian faith. By 1600, Universität Rostock was Lutheran affiliated). Nicolaus Wennicerus listed Lüdge in Westfalia as his hometown where he would have been known as Claas Wennitzer. Westfalia is just west of Lower Saxony. He would have spoken a dialect of German.

On the basis of all documents examined so far, Pastor Nicolaus is the only Claes who can be associated with the Marienhafe community during the childhood of Pieter Claessen. If Claes was the father, Pieter had to be only 5 years old or less when the pastor died in 1622. (This assumes that Pastor Nicolaus was not in Marienhafe before 1616, although it is possible that he had visited earlier). Young Pieter may have been orphaned in 1622, unless his mother somehow managed to survive the torturous destruction and economic turmoil of the Thirty Years War. Perhaps in the next generation, or when DNA profiles become more common than fingerprints, it will be possible to compare the DNA of Pieter Claessen descendants with descendants of the Wennitzer family in Westfalia. Meanwhile, this plausible, but imaginative, story must remain suspended in the status of an extended footnote without confirmatory evidence.

Concurrently during 1622, the year of Pastor Nicolaus' demise and for two years after, Brookmerland was ransacked and burned by the mercenary army of the Graf of Mansfeld, one of the more destructive

---

[14] Peter Fridrich Reershemius, *Ostfriesländisches Prediger-Denkmahl* (Aurich 1796), p.177.

campaigns of the Thirty Years War between Catholics and Protestants. Tileman Dothias Wiarda wrote in his Ostfriesischen Geschichte (Aurich 1794)[15] that 33 houses in Marienhafe had been burned down or destroyed and abandoned while only 9 houses were left standing. There could have been many orphans in the Marienhafe area after 1624.[16] As to how these conditions affected the youth of Pieter Claessen in Marienhafe remains speculative, but they surely provide a realistic context that is more relevant than the fictitious account of Pieter being born to Margaret van der Goes and Claes Cornelissen van Schouw in the Netherlands or on the Swedish island of Boda.

As Charles Hoppin wrote in "Pieter Claesen van Norden and the Wyckoffs" (1932), Pieter's beginnings in New Netherland "have no connection whatever with the life of Claes Cornelissen van Schouw, whom some Wyckoffs have erroneously proclaimed as the father of Pieter Claesen van Norden..."[17] Hoppin proceeded through the Pieter Niclaesen accounts in the Rensselaerswyck papers and anything relevant in the 15 volumes of *Documents Relating to the Colonial History of the State of New York*, finding nothing remotely suggesting any connection to Claes Cornelissen van Schouw (from the Netherlands). Pieter Niclaesen (Claessen) did not come to New Netherland on the same boat as Claes Corneliszen, and their names never appear on the same page in the voluminous pages of the *Van Rensselaer Bowier Manuscripts* spanning 1630-1643. Claes Corneliszen first appears in colonial documents in 1640, not in Rensselaerswyk, but in New Amsterdam. His first child was baptized in New Amsterdam when Pieter Claessen was a mature young man. As William J. Hoffman pointed out in the *The American Genealogist* (1945), Pieter Claessen (Wyckoff) never appeared as a sponsor for any

---

15 Tileman Dothias Wiarda, *Ostfriesischen Geschichte* (Aurich 1794). Vol. 15, pp. 202-203

16 Anyone who has seen the drama *Mutter Courage und Ihre Kinder* by Bertolt Brecht, in German or English translation, will understand something of the horrible devastation, dilemmas, and suffering endured by a single mother just trying to keep herself and her children alive.

17 Charles A. Hoppin, "Pieter Claesen van Norden and the Wyckoffs," in *The Washington Ancestry, and Records of Forty Other Colonial American Families, 3 vols. 1932 (Greenfield, Ohio.: 3: 102).*

of the 7 children born to Corneliszen and baptized in New Netherland,[18] even though they lived only a few miles apart for most of their lives in the vicinity of New Amsterdam. Knowing the significance of recording family participation at life's significant events in 17th century Christian culture, it would be unthinkable that Pieter would not attend any of these baptisms if Pieter was related to Claes Corneliszen whose children would have been his siblings. We can only infer that Pieter Claessen was not related to Corneliszen and was neither a native of the Netherlands nor of Böda in Sweden,[19] but came from a vicinity that was to become part of modern Germany. There can be little doubt that the majority of the Wyckoffs of America descend from Pieter Claessen who came from the area of Norden, Ostfriesland, and was indentured for six years beginning in 1637 on the estate of Kiliean van Rensselaer, at Papscanee Island toward the east side of the Hudson River, nearly opposite Fort Orange (Albany, N.Y.).[20] Here the young immigrant Pieter Claessen worked under the supervision of a fellow Frisian speaker, Simon Walichsz. who had been a fellow passenger on the same ship to the New World.

---

[18] William J. Hoffman, "Claes Cornelissen van Schouw(en), Meutelaer and the Wyckoff Ancestry," *The American Genealogist* 86, Vol. XXII, No. 2 (October 1945): 66.

[19] Both were mentioned as likely possibilities for a son of Captain Claes Corneliszen in *The Old World Progenitors of the Wyckoff Family: A Genealogy.* Prepared from the Manuscript Genealogical Collections of the late William Forman Wyckoff of Jamaica, New York . Edited and published by William LeRoy Wyckoff and Herbert James Wyckoff, 1936.

[20] On the quality and extent of documentation, see last section below, Notes on Wyckoff Documentary History, p. 47. The primary sources for early settlers in the Rensselaerswyck colony were most thoroughly examined by Van Laer, as listed below. The secondary sources which correctly interpret and supplement the work of Van Laer are also very useful.

A.J.F. Van Laer, *Van Rensselaer Bowier Manuscripts, being the letters of Kiliaen van Rensselaer, 1630-1643, and other documents relating to the colony of Rensselaerswyck.* (Albany: New York State Library, 1908): 810, 815.

"Deutsche Einzeleinwanderer und Familien in Neu-Niederland," *Jahrbuch fuur Auslanddeutsche Sippenkunde,* vol. 1 (1936): 45-53. In the yearbook of German emigrant kinship studies, Peter Klasen van Norden in Ostfriesland was listed as one among the German settlers of New Netherland. Pieter Clasz from Norden in Germany is also mentioned again as a 1637 passenger on the ship Rensselaerswyck in *Ship Passenger Lists: New York and New Jersey (1600-1825),* compiled and published by Carl Boyer III, in 1978.

The original Rensselaerswyck documents, as translated and interpreted by A.J.F. Van Laer, suggest that Nordingen was most likely a Dutch variant of Nordingerland, inferring that Pieter was from the area of Norden rather than from the town itself. A.J.F. van Laer had no reason to doubt that Pieter was from Nordingen in Ostfriesland, but did not realize in 1908 that there was a Wykhof estate (see Figs.2, 3) about 6 miles south of the town of Norden. Pieter Claessen had ventured forth to Amsterdam from his home, most likely a property designated as The Wykhof or Wiekhof on a canal leading to Marienhafe (see map, Fig. 8, p. 39), which by the 17th century lay east of Leybucht, the bay of the Ems River south of the city of Norden in Ostfriesland.[21] The family home of Pieter Claessen was not in the Netherlands, although according to David S. Cohen, there was "little difference either in language or house types between peasants in Friesland in the Netherlands and those in East Friesland in Germany."[22] Although Frisians are often classified as Dutch or German, their language and maritime culture along the North Sea coast endured and set them apart for many centuries. West Friesland, where a dialect of the Frisian language is still spoken in the region surrounding Groningen in the Netherlands, is on the west side of the Ems River. Ostfrisian, spoken by Pieter Claessen, is now extinct although a few Frisian archaicisms are retained in the Plattdeutsch (a Lower Saxon dialect of German) still spoken in Saterland, just south of Ostfriesland. (See Fig. 1, p. 18). Nordfrisian is still spoken by inhabitants of a few islands along the west coast of Denmark's Jutland peninsula and on the nearby mainland of Schleswig-Holstein, Germany. (See Fig. 7, p. 31). Wyk auf Föhr is the name of the harbor on one of the Nordfrisian islands and is now included in Germany. It was from this region that the Danish Vikings competed against their Norse brethren and conquered Dublin, Ireland in AD 851.

A second Wykhoff estate, also in Ostfriesland is located near Borsum, just south of Emden. (Both Marienhafe and Emden are located on the east side of the Ems River Bay. See . Fig. 1, p. 18). Many Wykhoffs now living throughout Niedersachsen (Lower Saxony) trace

[21] Today one can drive from Schiffsleidingsweg, 26529 Upgant-Schott, Germany (Wykhof near Norden) to Amsterdam in little over 3 hours. In 1636, it may have been more advantageous to sail by boat.

[22] David Steven Cohen, "How Dutch Were the Dutch of New Netherland?" *New York History* 62 (1981): 49. Cohen is also the author of *The Dutch-American Farm* (New York University Press, 1992).

their ancestors to this site.[23] Another family with the surname emigrated to Austria where their Wickhoff descendants remain very much aware of their Frisian origins.[24] There was one Anna Wyckoff from Austria who was naturalized as a U.S. citizen in 1925. The pretentious coat of arms fashioned for this branch of the Wickhoff family in Pomerania and carried into Austria depicts a manor surrounded by a high wall with water running past, an image which is much in keeping with the meaning of a settlement on a waterway. Most of this detailed information regarding Frisian origins was communicated to the Wyckoff family of America in the 1988 Anniversary Issue of the Wyckoff *Bulletin* which celebrated the arrival of Pieter Claessen 350 years earlier.[25] Descendants of Pieter Claessen Wyckoff in America can be forever grateful to Wilhelm J. Wykhoff and the late Hans Schrader of the German Wykhoff Association for the immense amount of time and effort expended in researching and documenting the European background of the American Wyckoff family. While Wilhelm Wyckoff and Hans Schrader spoke of a "theory" of Wyckoff origins, the preponderance of evidence cumulated here testifies to the "fact" that Pieter Claessen was definitely not Dutch, but emigrated from his home in Ostfriesland.

While the majority of Wyckoffs in America may be descended from Pieter Claessen from Wykhof near Marianhafe, there were some later Wyckoffs, with variant name spellings, who also came from

---

[23] Wilhelm J Wykhoff., *Die Geschichte der Familie Wykhoff.* Scharnebeck: Selbstverlag. 2008. While Americans have been unaware of their German cousins, German Wykhoffs have been aware of Wyckoffs in America throughout the 20th century. The German family origin of Frank Wykoff was recognized in the 1936 Berlin Olympics. In 1976, Wilhelm J. Wykhoff initiated a telephone conversation with Lou Ann Wyckoff, the American opera diva who was performing throughout Europe. The Wykhoff family reunions were inspired by those of the Wyckoff Association of America and were initiated in Germany in 1977.

[24] Hoppin, 1932, p. 123. Hans Schrader and his wife, Grace, invested considerable time, money, and travel to establish personal contacts with descendants, and outline the genealogy, of the Austrian branch of the Wykhoff family.

[25] Wilhelm Wykhoff, "An East Frisian Theory of Wyckoff Origins," *Bulletin of the Wyckoff House & Association, 350th Anniversary Issue, vol. LI.* (New York: Wyckoff Association, 1988): 9-21. A slide show of 115 transparencies was shown by Wilhelm Wykhoff at a Wyckoff Association anniversary dinner in 1988. I have recommended that these slides be digitized on a CD and offered for sale in the Wyckoff country store.

Germany. An index to passenger lists of ships arriving at the port of New York from foreign ports from 1820 to 1957 lists over 1400 Wyckoffs, Wiekhoffs, et al. There are none who spelled the name Wijcoff or Wijckoff and none who reported a residence in the Netherlands. Most of the Wyckoffs were Americans travelling overseas, and I find myself included on the list. The only other nationality of Wyckoff passengers represented was German. Heinrich Wycoff, born 12 Feb. 1845 in Westphalia, came to the U.S. in 1866 and lived in Nebraska, Illinois, and Missouri. Louisa Wyckoff, born about 1815 arrived on 1 Oct. 1855. Johann Hinrich Wieckhoff, born 11 Dec.1839 in Poggenwurth (or Dithmarschen in Schleswig-Holstein) sailed on the ship, Herder, and arrived in America with his wife, Anna Diers, and 4 children, Emma 19, Claus 16, Heinrich 8, and Grete 7 on 23 May 1882.[26] Alfred Wyckoff arrived from Germany in 1908. Phillip Wyckoff arrived from Germany in 1932. From 1925 to 1938, there were German arrivals named Wieckhoff, Wickhoff, Weckhauf and Wehkhoff.[27] The mother of the Wykhoff genealogist, Hans Schrader, was not listed by her maiden name, but her brother, Gerhard Wiekhoff was. The task remains to determine how many of these German passengers immigrated or became permanent residents, but the bottom line is that the name was not invented in America; and not all Wyckoffs in America are descended from Pieter Claessen. The majority of Ostfriesian emigrants to the U.S. came in the 19th century and settled in the Midwest.[28] It should not be surprising to find a few Wykoffs among them.

Gerhard Henry Wyckoff, a NYC fireman. was born on 26 September 1875 in Jersey City, N.J. His father was George Kasjen Wyckoff, a brewer in Lütetsburg, Ostfriesland. There was one Wladyslav Wyckoff from Russia who was naturalized in 1897. [I met one Russian Waychoff in the 1970s who was employed at Cornell University, and it is obvious that the —off sounding suffix, as in Romanoff and Chekhov,

---

[26] This information on the names and ages of wife and children was provided to me recently (2013) on an ancestral chart sent by Harald Wiekhoff of Schleswig, Germany. I expect that many Wyckoff descendants who are finding it difficult to trace their descent from Pieter Claessen may want to consider various spellings of other, later Wyckoff immigrants from Germany.

[27] *New York, Passenger Lists, 1820-1957* [database on-line]. Provo, UT, USA: Ancestry.com Operations, Inc., 2010.

[28] An active website for those who have ancestors from East Frisia can be found by searching on internet for OGSA (Ostfrisian Genealogical Society of America).

is a genitive ending in Russian, and has no common meaning and no genetic relationship to Germanic –hof]. Yet according to some self-appointed authority on wikipedia.com (last modified 19 March 2013), all persons in America with the surname Wyckoff and all its spelling variations can be traced to the family of Pieter Claessen.

The highest concentration of Wykhoffs in modern Europe, according to census data and telephone directories are in the German province of Niedersachsen (Lower Saxony) which includes Ostfriesland, with Schleswig-Holstein (bordering on Denmark) a distant second. It has not yet been determined if the Wykhoffs of Schleswig-Holstein derive from the Wykhof estate near Marienhafe or The Wykhof near Borsum. Since the bays and canals of the eastern Schleswig area connect to the Baltic Sea, it is entirely possible that yet another ancient settlement on a bay or waterway went by the name of The Wykhoff, but has disappeared. However, it should be noted that a Wyk (or Wik) settlement dating from the 13th century was located near Kiel. Wik is now a northern district of Kiel, which is the major German naval port on the Baltic Sea. The Wickhoffs of Austria trace their Frisian origin to Pomerania which is just east of Schleswig. Wiek, or Wieck, is a town in the Rügen district of Pomerania bordered on all sides by the Baltic Sea. Rügen is the only district in Germany that consists entirely of islands.

Through an online surname mapping program, many Wykhoff families can now be found in the cities: Berlin, Hamburg, Bremen, et al.[29] While it is possible that isolated Wyckoff families may have migrated to other parts of Germany and the Netherlands, their ancestors, and those of any of their descendants who emigrated to America in the 19th century, probably originated in Friesland. A recent search for the compound Wijckoff and several spelling variants at Nederlandse Familienamenbank, the primary Dutch surname search website, yielded no result, although there were 33 named Van der Wijk. (Fortunately, members of the Wyckoff Association have disavowed any familial relationship with Van Wijk and its associated coat of arms).[30]

---

[29] See Geogen Surname Mapping at
http://christoph.stoepel.net/geogen/en/Default.aspx.
[30]   Several online family crest and heraldry stores will sell flags, wall plaques, and surname history on parchment scroll ($67.98 with bronze frame at ArmorCrests). "If your name does not show up in our search, please place an order anyways, and we will research it for you." (4crest.com). Several years ago, I saw another framed coat of arms hanging on the wall of a distant cousin. Now you can download a readily available Wyckoff Coat of Arms in color for only $12.75. Rings for $235, and even useful mousepads and mugs decorated

Whether spelled *wijk* or *wyck*, neither the Dutch usage of the term in the proper name, Van der Wijk, nor in the place name, Rensselaerswyck, connotes a location on a bay. Van Wyck is a Dutch name; Wykhof is Frisian. If there are, or ever have been, any Wyckoffs in Holland, they most likely originated in Friesland, just as surely as anyone with the surname Van Ness must have an ancestor who originated in the town of Nes on the Friesian island of Ameland.

The Frisians were long characterized as seafaring traders and dairy farmers. It is significant that the world's most productive breed of dairy cattle is the black & white Holstein-Friesian, and most of the Wykhoffs living in modern Europe still reside in the region of Germany in proximity to Denmark and Lower Saxony, but it seems safe to assume that very few contemporary Wyckoffs, whether found in Germany, America, Austria, or the Netherlands, could still be employed in sea trading or dairy farming. The earlier meaning and history of their Frisian surname has undoubtedly been lost to many of them. In common everyday usage, it is enough to understand the functional identification purpose of the surname.

Friesland, where our Wyckoff name originated, has not been a national political entity in the modern era. Friesland is a cultural and linguistic area lying around the southeast coasts of the North Sea. (See Fig.1, & Fig. 7, p. 31). It has at times been under the jurisdictions of the modern states of Denmark, Germany, and the Netherlands. At the time of Pieter Claessen's birth in the 17th century, there was no modern nation-state of Germany, which came about only very late in the 19th century, a political accomplishment attributed to the nationalistic Franco Prussian War promoted by Otto von Bismarck. As part of the Holy Roman Empire (see map, Fig. 6, p. 28), Friesland was only one among many sources of emigrants solicited by Holland for the settlement of New Netherland.

For centuries, the North Sea was labelled *Mare Frisicum* on the maps of non-Frisian geographers. Around 700 AD, the trading sphere

---

with family coat of arms can be purchased in short order. Gold and silver rings are coming soon for a price much cheaper than what Gustave Anjou was charging for his stories 100 years ago. But then, he was offering us royal blood while these contemporary entrepreneurs have us descend only from knights in shining armor. What you purchase from these modern shysters may not be the Brooklyn Bridge, but at least, you will have something tangible to show for your money!

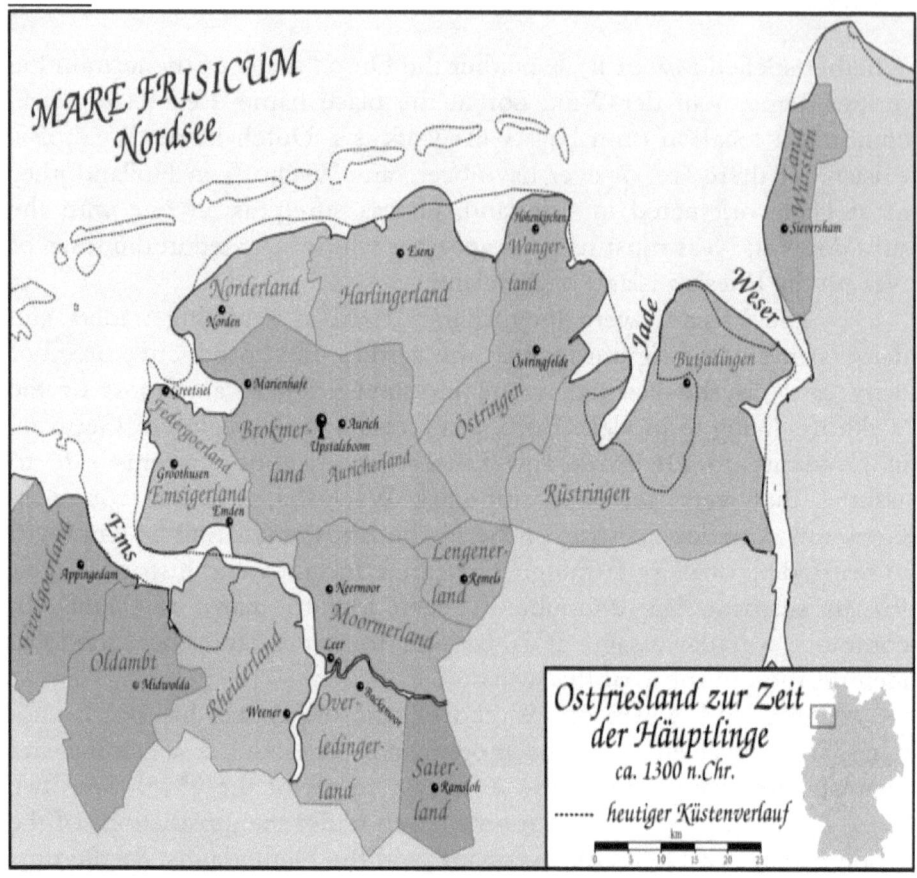

Figure 1. East Frisia at the time of the Chiefdoms, ca. 1300 AD (Maker: Onno Gabriel. based on several sources) 22 September 2007. http://wiki-en.genealogy.net/East_Frisia With the 1947-1950 construction of the Störtebeker dyke, the bay was reduced to its present size. The dotted lines approximate contemporary coastlines. Over the centuries, dikes have been built and much land has been reclaimed for farming. Note that the Frisian coastal islands were formerly submerged and the land just to the west of Marienhafe was formerly a bay. The first Wykhof house-barn near Marienhafe was constructed ca. 1250 AD Following the storm surges of 1374 and 1376, the bay stretched from Greetsiel in the west to Marienhafe in the east and to the edge of Norden in the north.

of the Frisians was very extensive. Dorestad (modern Duurstede) on a tributary of the Rhine River was an important Frisian trading center and issued its own coinage. The Frisian occupation of Dorestad predates, by centuries, the medieval castle built in the town of Wijk bij Duurstede. The castle and residence of a bishop has now been restored for tourism.

Zeichnung von Gerhard H. Janssen, Osteel.

Figure 2. Traditional Frisian House-barn at Osteel sketched by G. Janssen, between Marienhafe and Norden. Reprinted here by permission of Frau Nörtker, granddaughter and heiress to the late Gerhard Janssen, *1914 – 2005.*

      The original Wykhof house-barn built ca. 1250 AD near Marienhafe was probably indistinguishable from others in the general area (Fig. 2 above, Fig. 10, p. 46) but it was located on the Störtebeker Tief (waterway, see Fig. 8, p. 39) with access to the bay, and the place name was appropriately labeled with the *wyk-* word stem. How much is fact and how much is legend may not be determined precisely, but the famous pirate Claes Störtebeker has been closely associated with The Wykhof, the Marienkirche, and the regional chieftain's castle, now a bed and breakfast residence called Ulferts Börg. Störtebeker is said to have married a daughter of the local chieftain, and the legend persists that slippers reputedly worn by Störtebeker were preserved for a century or more in Ulferts Börg. They are now in the museum in Emden. The Wykhof house-barn (Fig. 3 below) located less than a mile west of Marienhafe was rebuilt in 1757 and burned in 1974. Today Marienhafe and the Wykhof estate are about 9 miles away from the bay, but it is well documented that there was a brief time just before AD 1400 when the Leybucht extended all the way to Marienkirche. Shortly after this, the water receded and The Wykoff was for a brief time actually at the edge of the bay. See Fig. 4, p. 22 below. As the bay retreated farther to the west, it was still at The Wykhof on the Störtebeker Tief (canal) that cargos from larger ships were unloaded and dispersed, or reloaded onto smaller boats for further transport into Marienhafe. (The location of Wykhof, or Wiekhof, relative to Marienhafe can be seen on Fig. 8, p. 39). It is more than likely that these historical and hydrological events were largely due to a natural climatic change affecting sea level along with incidences of seasonal flooding and storm surges; acting in combination with circumstantial factors of human ship architecture, especially the shallow draft of some sea-going vessels, and lack of flood control by contemporary dike-building technology.[31]

In succeeding centuries, the technology improved with the persistent effort to prevent catastrophic flooding and reclaim more farmland from the sea. The results for the Leybucht area can be seen in Fig. 4, p. 22. "Gott schuf das Meer. Der Frisie de Küste." (God created the sea. Frisians created the coastlines). Perhaps some credit should also be extended to the Frisian breed of horses which powered much of the dike construction.

---

[31] The hydrological events at the end of the 14th century correlate well with the storm floods accompanying the end of the Medieval Optimum and the onset of the Little Ice Age, a global climatic phenomenon. Inspired by *Times of Feast, Times of Famine* (1971) by LeRoy Ladurie, and then by *Climate: Present, Past, and Future* (1977) by Hubert Lamb, I outlined the effects of this global climatic change on prehistoric cultures in North America in a Cornell University Ph.D. dissertation, and later researched the documentary and proxy records of the synchronic effects in Chinese history.

The old Wykhoff (burned, 1974)

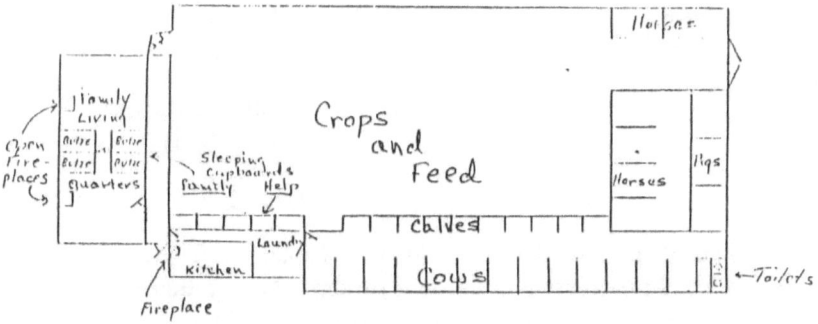

Figure 3. Modern aerial photograph, and floor plan of The Wykhof ca. 1840. Adapted from Wilhelm Wykhof, *Wyckoff Family Bulletin* 1988, p.14.

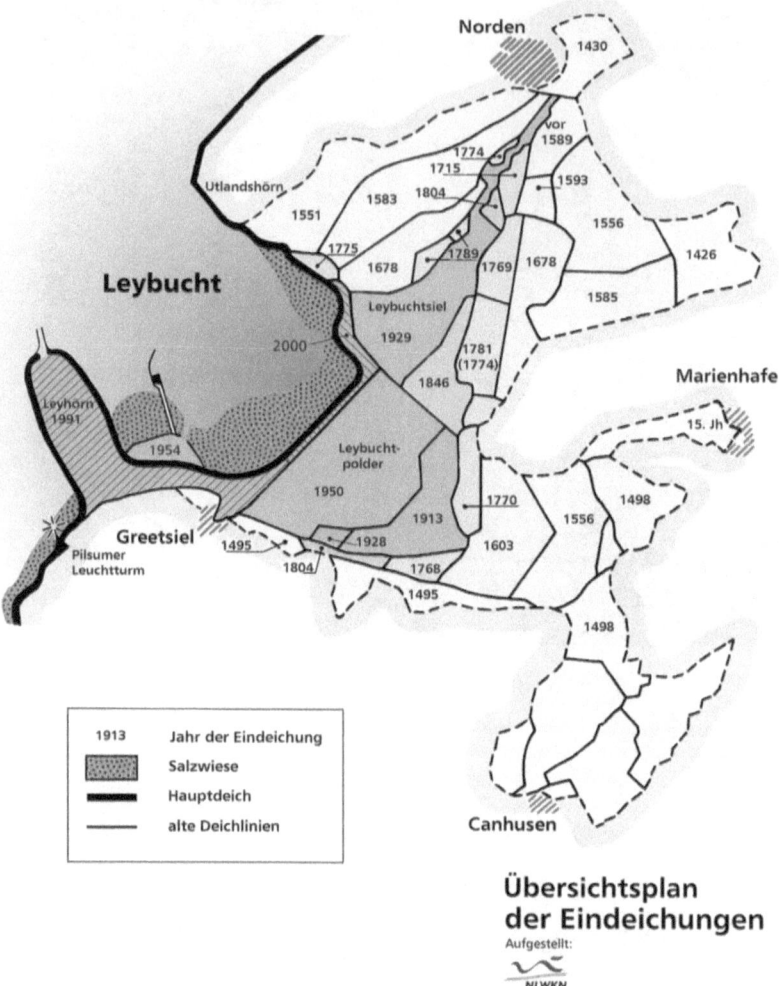

Die Leybucht in ihrer größten Ausdehnung
nach den Sturmfluten von 1362-1377
und die Eindeichungen bis heute

Norden
1430

vor 1589

1774
1715

Utlandshörn
1593

1583 1804

1551

1556

1775

1426

1678

1789

1769 1678

Leybucht

Leybuchtsiel

1585

2000

1929

1781
(1774)

1846

Marienhafe

Leyhörn
1991

15. Jh

1954

Leybucht-
polder

1950

1770

1556

1498

1913

Greetsiel

1495

1603

Pilsumer
Leuchtturm

1804

1928

1768

1495

1498

1913	Jahr der Eindeichung
	Salzwiese
	Hauptdeich
	alte Deichlinien

Canhusen

Übersichtsplan
der Eindeichungen
Aufgestellt:

NLWKN

Figure 4. Map of the Leybucht at its greatest expanse after the storm floods of 1362-1377 and its progressive diking until today. Notice that a narrow neck of water extends eastward toward Marienhafe ca. AD 1400. This was the Störtebeker Tief where The Wiekhof, can be seen on Fig. 8, p. 39, a map made ca. 1800. The distance from Norden to Marienhafe is about 6 miles. This map of the Leybucht, originally in color, was made by Hans Homeier for the Niedersächsicher Landesbetrieb für Wasserwirtschaft Küsten- und Naturschutz, Aurich. The NLWKN-Betriebstelle has graciously granted permission to reproduce this map.

Figure 5. Marienkirche in Marienhafe, ca. 1400 AD A Frisian sea-going Kogge (Cog) with a shallow draft such as might have been utilized by Claes Störtebeker, is seen docked near the walled-in Wik (settlement and marketplace) of Marienhafe. This painting represents an artistic rendering of Marienhafe during the abnormal and distinct climatic change at the end of the Medieval Climatic Optimum. Toward the end of the 15th century, the church had three naves and a six story tower. Today's remnant has only one nave and the tower has been reduced to 4 stories. The wall around Marienhave was taken away in 1557; the material used for construction elsewhere. This is a black and white cropping of the original 60cm by 90cm oil painting by Gerhard H. Janssen depicted in color on the cover, It is based on a sketch by Harm Bents derived from a description by the historian Eggerik Beninga, 1490–1562. Permission to utilize the painting has been granted by the private owner.

Marienhafe with its prominent church steeple is easily recognized at a distance on the flat landscape; it is only about a half mile away from The Wyckoff. Both the church and house-barn originated ca. 1250 AD However briefly, both Marienhafe and The Wykoff were water transport terminals at one time. Even if Störtebeker was never hosted in The Wykhof, he had to pass by as his cogs unloaded cargo at the wharf at Marienhafe. Reputedly, Störtebeker was a benefactor to Marienkirche. The Wykhoff was a household; Marienhafe hosted a Wik, an open marketplace near the church. Young Pieter Claessen had to be familiar with the town. His mother and godfather were probably members of families residing in or near Marienhafe. Pastor Niklaus resided in the Pastorenhaus next to the Marienkirche. from 1616 to 1622.

As passengers from Friesland on the Rensselaerswyk in 1636-37,[32] Pieter Claessen and Simon Walichsz were accompanied by other immigrants from Norway, Sweden, and Pomerania. When the *Van Rensselaer Bowier Manuscripts* were translated and published in 1908, it was noted that the detailed list of settlers in the early colony "…throws much new light on the large proportion of elements other than Dutch that entered into the population of the colony."[33] When Joel Eno made a list of early New York Knickerbocker families in 1914, noting their place of origin and where they settled in New Netherland, he remarked that the settlements along the Hudson (including Manhattan), on Long Island, and in Northeastern Jersey were assumed to be Dutch, "…though drawn from the whole south coast of the North Sea."[34] When the first Walloon settlers arrived in New Amsterdam in 1624, the only non-indigenous permanent resident on Manhattan was Jan Rodrigues, a black creole who had come from the Caribbean on a Dutch ship in 1613. The pietist Walloon families established a few small farms north of Fort New Amsterdam. Although sponsored by the Dutch West India Company, the Walloons refused to speak Dutch or attend the Dutch Reformed Church, setting a pattern of non-assimilation into Dutch culture to be followed by successive waves of European immigrants. Cornelis Van Vorst, the Director of Pavonia, the first European settlement in New

---

[32] A.J.F. Van Laer, *Van Rensselaer Bowier Manuscripts*: 810, 815.

[33] A.J.F. Van Laer, *Van Rensselaer Bowier Manuscripts:* 33.

[34] Joel N. Eno, "New York 'Knickerbocker' Families, Origin and Settlement," *New York Genealogical and Biographical Record* (NYGBR) 45 (1919): 387.

Jersey, spoke a variety of French, as did all the other Walloon refugees who made up most of the early settlers in New Netherland. Richard Schemerhoorn, in a deliberate attempt to locate more exact European origins of early Dutch settlers, noted in 1934 that "a great many of those who are assumed to be Dutch, actually came from what later became sections of Germany. The latter were principally the independent duchies or principalities of Oldenburg, Hanover, Rhine Province, Westphalen, and Schleswig-Holstein."[35] Settlers from Emden and Norden were obviously Ostfrisian. Schermerhoorn also noted individuals from Norway, Denmark and Finland. In 1643, when the Jesuit Father Isaac Jogues escaped from the Mohawks and passed through New Amsterdam, he was impressed by the international character of the settlement and wrote in his journal that there could be 4 or 5 hundred men of different sects or nations. He was told by the Director-General that 18 languages were spoken in Manhattan.[36] Undoubtedly, one of those languages was Frisian. The Dutch were intent on acquiring permanent settlers to compete against the more populous English settlements of New England. New Englanders had already displaced a Dutch settlement in Connecticut. There was also a significant community of English immigrants living in the midst of New Amsterdam who refused to speak Dutch and worship in the Reformed Church. After 1650, members of non-Reformed congregations were allowed to have their own places of worship.

While family members of non-Dutch settlements remained separate from Dutch culture, single immigrants often took Dutch brides. In scanning the marriages recorded after 1639 in the Reformed Dutch Church, New York, Joyce Goodfriend mentions "Bridegrooms came from Hersberg in Silesien, Brandtfort in Scholtlant, Hamburg, Tonsbergen in Noordwegen, Stockholm, de Provincie van Essex, de Provincie van Hertfort, de Provincie van Sutfulck, Novan in

---

35 Richard Schemerhoorn, Jr., "Representative Pioneer Settlers of New Netherland and Their Original Home Places," *New York Biographical and Genealogical Record 65* (1934): 2-12. Schermerhoorn listed immigrants from West Friesland as Dutch.

36 It seems only fitting that a naturalization ceremony for new immigrants was held on the lawn at the Wyckoff House in Brooklyn in conjunction with the 2002 annual Wyckoff family reunion. In addition to the African and European languages spoken around the tent, my wife, Lydia Wykoff, and I were privileged to hear her native Chinese spoken by some of the latest immigrants.

Vranckryck, Cascalis in Portugal, Westeraes in Sweden Noordwegen, Conigsbergen in Pruysen, and Bristol in Engelant."[37] Portugal, Scotland, Norway, France, Sweden, England, and many German provinces surely attest to the extensive international intercourse met in New Netherland.[38] Italy, West Africa, and the Caribbean could be added to sources of the non-Dutch population in New Amsterdam. Jan de Fries, the son of Johan de Fries, a Dutch sea captain and a black woman, was baptized Christian on 25 August 1647, married Ariantje Dircks of Albany in the Reformed Church where his four children were also baptized. Later he became an original patentee of Tappan, New Jersey where his descendants lived for several generations. Anthony Jansen van Vaes, a mullato who arrived in New Amsterdam as a free person, defended his rights, married a Dutch woman, and was the first non-indigenous person to live at Gravesend on Long Island.[39]

The first generation children of the bridegrooms coming from the international (non-Dutch) population of immigrants were usually baptized in the Dutch Reformed Church and were counted as Dutch. Although they lived only briefly under Dutch rule before the English took over the colonies, it is surprising that the Dutch language persisted in the Reformed Church as long as it did, but that was primarily in rural New Jersey. The Dutch Reformed churches came to resemble the English churches, although they had fewer exterior architectural

---

[37] Joyce Goodfriend, "Foreigners in a Dutch Colonial City," *New York History* 90.4 (Fall 2009), pp, 243-244, citing information from *Collections of the New York Genealogical and Biographical Society*, Vol. 1 (1890).

[38] Elsewhere, Goodfriend has emphasized a second stream of immigration in the Dutch trade from West Africa and the Caribbean. 41% of New York City households owned slaves by 1703. Joyce D. Goodfriend, "Burghers and Blacks: The Evolution of a Slave Society at New Amsterdam," *New York History*, 59 (1978): 125-44. Many black couples from Curacao were married and their babies baptized in the Reformed Dutch Church of New York.

[39] *Graham Russell Hodges, Root & Branch: African Americans in New York & East New Jersey, 1613-1863.* Chapel Hill: University of North Carolina. 1999: 11-12. Unfortunately, later slaves coming directly from West Africa found it much more difficult to be baptized in the Reformed Church, and their masters were much less willing to sponsor baptisms or to free them.

embellishments.[40] The Reformed Church of America dropped "Dutch" from its title in 1867. Many of the second and third generation Dutch immigrants were being married in Methodist, Presbyterian, Congregational, and Episcopal churches. Although the Rev. Isaac N. Wyckoff of the Dutch Reformed Church in Albany, N.Y. had assisted the immigration of a few Dutch settlers to Midwestern states, promoted by Van Raalte in the mid-nineteenth century, the numbers of Dutch immigrants were negligible when compared to the numbers for German, Irish, and Italian immigrants to the U.S. Already when New Netherland became New York in 1664, as much as one-third of the population of the Dutch colony actually came from northern German towns and principalities. (Numbers of English and other non-Dutch settlers were here counted among the Dutch majority).

In the 1981 article, "How Dutch Were the Dutch of New Netherland?" David S. Cohen of the New Jersey Historical Commission determined exact origins for 904 settlers who immigrated to New Netherland in the 17th century. About half of them (445) came from states other than the Netherlands, the largest contingent coming from surrounding principalities of Germany, but many others coming from Norway, Sweden, Denmark, France, Belgium, et al. As he notes, too many earlier accounts of New Netherland settler origins "have been either filio-pietistic genealogies of purely antiquarian interest, or exercises in ethnic chauvinism."[41]

Cohen's analysis is restricted to immigrants coming primarily on Dutch ships. Historians must utilize whatever data exist. If there had been scientific samples of the whole New Netherland population who had arrived on earlier non-Dutch ships, the Dutch element would have been even less significant. There were already many English living among the Dutch residents. Not only did the English attend their own churches, but the names of their settlements, Hempstead, Jamaica, Newtown, Flushing, et al. were English. The number of locally born New Netherlanders baptized in Dutch Reformed churches were often only half Dutch, although they were usually counted as Dutch.

---

[40] Adrian C. Leiby, *The Early Dutch and Swedish Settlers of New Jersey.* Princeton, N.J.: D. Van Nostrand Company, Inc. 1964.

[41] David Steven Cohen, "How Dutch Were the Dutch of New Netherland?" *New York History* 62 (1981): 49.

Europe in the mid seventeenth century. Map by Adele L. Johnson.

Figure 6. European sources of immigration to New Netherland. Map reproduced from David Steven Cohen, "How Dutch Were the Dutch of New Netherland?" *New York History* 62 (1981): 50. Permission to publish here granted by New York State Historical Association Library, Cooperstown, NY.

Descendants of New Netherland settlers need to conceptualize their ancestral homelands pluralistically. A single map of the homeland that is confined to modern Holland, such as one sees in most books about New Netherland,[42] will not suffice. A map (Fig. 6 above) that embraces much of northern Europe in the 17th century is most appropriate for New Netherland descendants.

In the highly recommended book, *New Netherland Roots*,[43] the author, a non-certified but competent genealogist, was initially motivated to find the place of origin for her immigrant ancestor from Holland. After years of toil and effort, she was finally able to visit the birthplace of Coenradt ten Eyck in Moers, Germany, not Holland. In her Introduction, she writes:

> The popular image of the people who came out with the Dutch West India Company is that most of them were "Dutch," but research in both European and American records proves many were refugees to the Netherlands from what is now Belgium, Germany, France, Scandinavia, and Great Britain. Therefore the researcher may lose a "Dutch" ancestor or two in the research process, but gain a more varied ancestry. (p. xiii).

In her Conclusion, writing from Salt Lake City, Epperson states that family history ultimately teaches us that we are all part of one huge family, and as artificial boundaries disappear, it could become anathema to war against nations of relatives. "Then there will be peace on earth, good will to men." (p. 105).

Frisians (including those from West, East, and North Frisia) comprised a significant non-Dutch speaking ethnic group in New Amsterdam. Van Laer mentioned a Berend Dirksen from Norden who was in New Amsterdam in 1639. Frederick Philipse was born in the small Frisian town of Bolswaert. He immigrated as a carpenter in 1647, married a wealthy widow and became the landlord of the expansive

---

[42]   For example, a recent (2009) book published by Cornell University Press, *The Colony of New Netherland: A Dutch Settlement in Seventeenth-Century America*, by a Dutchman, Jaap Jacobs, shows only a map of his home country (p. 34). Although Jacobs acknowledges the considerable number of English transmigrants among the Dutch in New Netherland, he omits mention of other groups of non-Dutch settlers in New Amsterdam (pp. 50, 268).

[43]   Gwenn F. Epperson, *New Netherland Roots*. (Baltimore: Genealogical Publishing Company. 1994).

Philipsburg Manor. Captain David Peterszoon de Vries built Fort Vriesendael in an attempt to establish and protect a settlement near present day Tappen. Jonas Bronk was the leader of a North Frisian group of settlers who carried out one of the first well-prepared and thoroughly organized permanent settlements in New Netherland. Bronk himself was neither Dutch nor Frisian, but probably came from an island between Sweden and Denmark. Pieter Stuyvesant de Fries, a Director General of New Amsterdam, may have spoken Dutch but his native language was Frisian; he was born in Pepenga, Friesland. The father-in-law of Pieter Claessen was originally from the village of Nes on the Frisian island of Ameland before he moved to Vianan. While the maternal ancestry of Grietje Van Nes, the wife of Pieter Claessen, was of a middle class family (Van der Burchgraeff) from South Holland,[44] her father, Cornelis Hendrick van Ness, was from West Friesland and probably spoke Frisian with Pieter Claessen. Both Grietje's last name (Van Nes) and Pieter Claessen's last name (Wykhof) are 100% Frisian. In Mendelian terms, the genetic heritage of the first generation children of Pieter Claessen Wyckoff and Grietje Van Nes was ¾ Friesian. Although many descendants of Pieter Claessen were baptized in the Dutch Reformed Church in New York and New Jersey, their genetic makeup was very mixed from the beginning. The minority languages of the original settlers, including Frisian, and French, were abandoned within a few generations. Nicholas, the first son of Pieter Claessen, married Sara Monfoort, the daughter of Pieter Monfoort, a French

---

[44] William J. Hoffman, "An Armory of American Families of Dutch Descent," *New York Genealogical and Biographical Record* 72 (1941): 148-155. Hoffman was an accomplished genealogist who utilized Netherlands documents to research the Van Ness family in Holland and America. He noted that Grietje Van Ness married "Pieter Claes Wyckhof from Nordigen, East Friesland." Hoffman's work provides valuable information for researching the maternal Dutch origins of the American Wyckoff family which is too often neglected in our cultural patronymic milieu. Hopefully, future members of the Wyckoff family with the XX chromosomal pattern will take up the challenge to gather mtDNA (mitochondrial DNA) data and increase our knowledge of our Dutch heritage. The Holland Society of New York strongly encourages information on DNA testing on their website: http://www.hollandsociety.com/holland-society-dna-project.html One surname example listed in their promotional material is Van Husum from Husum, Denmark, demonstrating an awareness that immigrants to New Netherland were not only of Dutch ancestry.

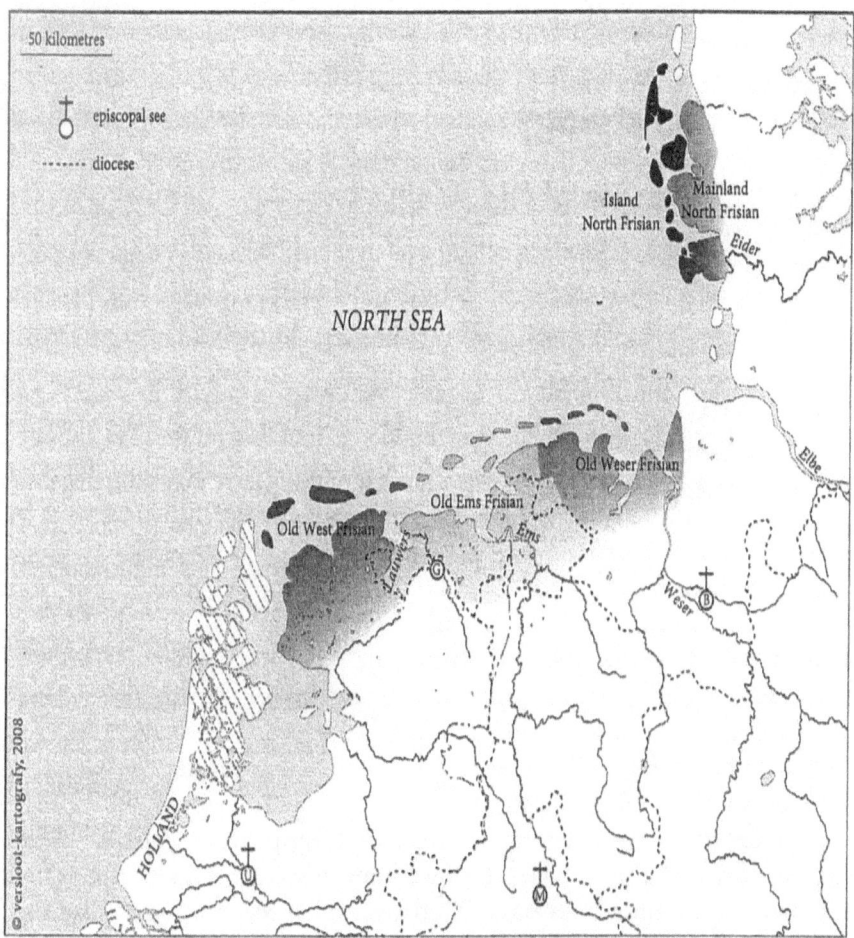

Figure 7. The geographical distribution of Frisian around 1300 in relation to the dioceses. U = Utrecht, M = Münster, B = Bremen. G = Groningen (added for orientation). The original Wykhof house-barn, built around 1250 AD was located within the dialect area of Old Ems Frisian. Old Ems and Old Weser Frisian together comprise Ost Frisian. Rolf H. Bremmer, Jr., *An Introduction to Old Frisian,* (Amsterdam: John Benjamins Publishing Company, 2009), 110. Permission to reproduce granted by Rights & Royalties Department, John Benjamins Publishing Co.

Huguenot.. The Wyckoff family, like those of the other immigrants, assimilated into the international New Amsterdam culture. Many of their immediate descendants intermarried with Dutch families near Brooklyn, N.Y., and subsequently spoke Dutch and English as succeeding generations moved on to New Jersey.

The widely disseminated advertisements promulgated by patroons throughout Europe stipulating "Freedoms and Exemptions" for potential colonists were apparently successful, especially in German provinces. In 1635, there was a plague which created many orphans who emigrated, but Pieter Claessen was not the first laborer to emigrate from Ostfriesland to New Netherland.[45] On the 26th of April, 1634, Hendrick Carstensz van Norden was engaged as a 21-year-old farm laborer to serve Henrick Conduit of Königsberg, East Prussia, or his agent in Rensselaerswyck for a period of four years. He was promised an annual salary of 10 rix-dollars, and his passage was paid in advance.[46] Two years later, Pieter was to receive a man's wages of 50 guilders per year for the first three years, and 75 guilders per year during the last four years of his indenture.[47] Evidently, his passage was also paid as part of the deal, although if he was an orphan he may have been eligible for government-paid emigration transport. A few workers in their late teens were occasionally accepted, but the patroons much preferred healthy, mature, able-bodied men who could start to work immediately. Labor was scarce in the colony, and the patroons were willing to increase salaries over time to prevent experienced employees from seeking greener pastures. If Pieter Claessen had been born in 1625 as the son of Claes Corneliszen, he would have been only 11 years old when he sailed for New Amsterdam. This is highly unlikely, but more significantly, there is no known birth record that can be validly assigned to the immigrant Pieter Claessen Wyckoff; and no church record of baptism has survived. Whenever available, church records should certainly be consulted, but cannot be reliably expected to survive over centuries. It seems most likely that Pieter was born ca. 1618.

Sometimes the most a genealogist can hope for is to discover the place of origin. We now know that Pieter Claessen came from Norden in East Friesland; not from North Friesland off the coast of Denmark,

---

[45] Cohen (1981) lists 20 original settlers from Norden, Emden, and other East Friesland communities. (Table 2: 52-53).

[46] *Van Rensselaer Bowier Manuscripts*, (1908): 288.

[47] Hoppin (1932): 103.

and not from West Friesland which is part of the Netherlands. Most of northeastern Netherlands along the North Sea was formerly occupied by Frisians while Dutch speakers lived inland. See Fig. 7, p. 31. Today, Frisian is spoken in the Netherlands only in the coastal provinces west of the Ems River basin. The West Frisian language can still be heard on a radio station in the area around Groningen.

Meaning

Wykhof was the *place name* south of Norden in East Friesland, Germany, whence Pieter Claessen emigrated to the New World, sailing from Amsterdam in 1636 and arriving at New Amsterdam in 1637. There is no one multiple volume dictionary of the Frisian language comparable to successive editions of the OED (*Oxford English Dictionary*) which lists dated contextual quotes and meaning glosses. However, there are etymological dictionaries for all of the modern European languages. There are scattered documents from extinct languages such as Gothic, and there are reconstructed vocabularies for Indo-Germanic and Indo-European which have been compiled in lists or dictionaries.[48] The exact spatial and temporal provenances of historical changes in phonology, grammar, and meaning in all the Germanic languages are all but impossible to determine, but trends are nevertheless discernible over millennia. As the founder of semiotics and pragmatism, America's greatest philosopher, Charles S. Peirce, commented, "A symbol, once in being, spreads among the peoples. In use and in experience, its meaning grows. Such words as *force, law, wealth, marriage*, bear for us very different meanings from those they bore to our barbarous ancestors."[49] Words and their meanings also become obsolete and even fall into disuse. Surnames persist even when the meaning is lost.

When word roots are combined to form a compound word, the new word may take on connotations that differ from the original constituents. Thus the independent word *Wik* may not have the exact same meaning as *Wik*- when it is compounded with -hof. With that

---

[48] Two principal Germanic references are the multi-volume *Deutsches Wörterbuch von Jacob Grimm und Wilhelm Grimm* (1854) and the one volume *Etymologishes Wörterbuch der Deutschen Sprache* (1883) by Friedrich Kluge.

[49] *Collected Papers of Charles Sanders Peirce*, Harvard University Press, 1960. Vol. 2: 302.

caveat in mind, it is still very informative to consider the historical changes in meaning of all the constituents.

The general meaning of Germanic *hof*, the second word root in the compound Wykhof, denoted a yard around a dwelling place which was often enclosed by a fence or wall. As society evolved in complexity, the domain of the reference extended from the yard around a house or house-barn to spaces around other private and public buildings such as the manorial house of a nobleman, a prince, a bishop, or a communal building such as a church. The meaning was further expanded to include a public marketplace (often adjacent to a church) and eventually to an enclosed place of business.

Spellings of *hof* have varied over time and space. The history of Marienhafe provided me by Harm Bents is a case in point. Since Marienhafe was, at least for brief period around AD 1400, a harbor on the extended Leybucht, I was tempted to interpret *-hafe* as a port, as in Bremerhaven, Cuxhaven, and Wilhelmshaven, which are harbor towns in Lower Saxony. (Marienhafe is sometimes spelled Marienhave). However, Marienhafe was already in existence ca. AD 1250 when there was no adjacent bay with water transport present. In Latin it was referred to as "curia sancte Marie" which translates as "hof der heiligen Maria." It was recorded as *Marienhove* in 1398, *Marienhoff* in 1427, and *Marienhave* in 1437. Spelling variations also included *hof*, *-hoffe*, and *-houe*. Its current spelling *Marienhafe* became standard around 1735. Only through history do we learn that the original meaning of *hof* was not a harbor, but clearly refers to the area surrounding the church, which could include a Wik/Markt (market area). In fact, *hof* (yard) and *wik* (household or settlement) sometimes overlap in spatial reference.

The general and oldest meaning of Germanic *wik*, the first word root in *Wykhof*, was a large family household, which was further extended to embrace a settlement, or village. In North German, Old Frisian, and Old English, the meaning was applied primarily to settlements around bays or on major waterways. Old Norse *vik* meant a place on a 'bay, inlet, or small creek' referring either to fjords from which they came or to the creeks in which they landed and set up camps. The Frisian cognate was pronounced [vik] as in English *victory*. Spellings of the word root vary over time and from place to place; they include wik, wyk, wic, wich, wick, wiek, vik, vic, vyc, vig, et al. More basic than spellings, pronunciations and meanings of the term evolved differently in various dialects and languages. Even within English, it takes conscious effort to recognize the same root where it occurs in altered or borrowed forms, as in: Sandwich, Viking, and Reykjavik.

In Old English as in Altfriesich, *wik* often denoted a dairy farm household or a settlement on a bay or river or both. The English, Frisians, and Anglo-Saxons had much in common, both in languages and cultures. In fact, it is hard to distinguish the Friesians among the Angli who invaded England.[50] The extensive usage of *wik* derivatives in England are legion, dating from a time when Old English was spoken, i.e., centuries before the Viking attacks around AD 800. The precursor to London was Lundenvic. Southhampton was Hamwic. York was Eoferwic. Gipeswic became Ipswich.[51] The commercial nature of the medieval trading centers and the industrial revolution extended the meaning of *wik* as in Saltwich where salt production established a settlement more industrial than agricultural. (Salt was absolutely essential for preserving fish in the Atlantic and North Sea areas). In the case of *wik*, Old English and Old Frisian meanings and phonology seem closer to Old Norse than to Old Dutch and Old High German. The presence and influence of Frisian traders in England and all around *Mare Frisicum*, the North Sea, was pervasive and enduring. In certain English place-names, *wic* came to be associated with buildings utilized for store-houses and trading.[52]

There is textual evidence for a late borrowing of the word *vicinity* from Latin *vicinitas* into English. In addition to early Roman occupation and early translations from church Latin into English, there were later numerous Norse settlements along the coast of Great Britain. Thus, generic *wik* as spoken and written in England over two millennia has been derived from multiple sources. In modern compound English surnames, the root is frequently spelled Wick-; in modern Norwegian, it is usually spelled Wik-.

Several German and Dutch dictionaries list *wik* or *wic* as borrowed from Latin *vicus*. While an early wholesale loan of *wik* from Latin is plausible for continental German and Dutch, it is less likely in North German where the association with a bay is manifested in Wyk near Kiel, Wyk auf Föhr, Wiek on an island in Pomerania, Wykhof near Marienhafe, Wyk and Wykhof near Emden, and even in Reykjavik, Iceland. All the Icelanders I have queried are aware that the *–vik* in

---

[50] Theodor Siebs, *Zur Geschichte der Friesich-Englisch-Friesischen Sprache.* Halle: Max Niemeyer, 1889.

[51] Helen Clarke and Björn Ambrosiani, *Towns in the Viking Age* (Leicester: Leicester University Press 1991).

[52] Albert H. Smith, *English Place-Name Elements* (Cambridge University Press, 1956): 258.

Reykjavik refers to a settlement on a bay. The late Hans Schrader (pers. comm. 2003) also noted cognate surnames such as *Vikhof* along the Baltic coast of Sweden. Even if it can be shown that North German *wik* was sometimes borrowed from Latin *vicus* via classical Roman or later Christian written sources, the association with settlements on a bay remains a meaningful independent innovation. There is an additional connotation for a term spelled *Wieke* in an 1857 Ostfriesian dictionary denoting a deliberately engineered widening of a canal, principally to provide access to a dock or wharf for harboring boats and transporting goods.[53] [The maiden name of Hans Schrader's German mother who immigrated to America was Wiekhoff]. Archaeological evidence for an early widening of the canal at The Wykhof could be significant.

Another local connotation of Wykhof occurring in Frisian reference works and recently communicated to me by local historian Harm Bents of Marienhafe, is "a place of refuge or escape."[54] Such a harbor on a bay can be a refuge from a storm anywhere, but the extended meaning of escape is a particularly appropriate extension of the local meaning when applied to Marienhafe in the years preceding 1400 AD when the pirate Störtebeker and his crews found refuge here to escape the pursuit of the Hanseatic League shippers. Here we find, perhaps for the first time, the application of *Wykhof* not merely to the settlement on the bay (Leybucht), but to a uniquely protected area around Marienkirche. The Liekedeeler or Victualler Brothers (names for followers of Störtebeker) numbered as many as 800 and had to be sheltered. The meaning of Wyk as a settlement on a waterway is here extended to refer to the space around the church where crews and stolen goods were protected inside a wall. Whether this precise meaning of *Wykhof* was widely disseminated before this time is doubtful. If a multivolume dictionary for Frisian comparable to the OED (*Oxford English Dictionary*) is ever compiled, we may be able to speak more definitively, but I have not noticed this connotative meaning of escape or refuge explicitly featured as an alternate meaning of *Wik* or *Wykhof* in

---

[53] C. Heinrich Stürenburg, *Ostfriesisches Wörterbuch* (Aurich: Carl Otto Sende, 1857): 330.

[54] Sources quoted by Harm Bents: Arend Remmers, *Von Aaltukerei bis Zwischenmooren. Die Siedlungsnamen zwischen Dollart und Jade,* (Leer 2004): 249, 262; Jan ten Doornkaat Koolman, *Wörterbuch der ostfriesischen Sprache, Norden 1879 bis 1884,* Bd. 3, S. 548, Bd. 2, S. 133; Cirk Heinrich Stürenburg, *Ostfriesisches Wörterbuch, Nachdruck der Ausgabe Aurich 1857,* (Leer 1996):330; and Ulrich Scheuermann, *Flurnamenforschung. Bausteine zur Heimat- und Regionalgeschichte,* (Melle 1995): 126.

dictionaries of other northern Germanic languages, or even in glossaries of West or North Frisian.

The Marienhafe church is curiously appropriate for such an interpretation if the legend is true that the building served as a safe haven for the famous pirate, and locally celebrated Störtebeker. He and his allies succeeded in sacking and burning Bergen, the principal city of Norway in 1392. For a time afterward, even the great herring fishing fleets on the North Sea were afraid to sail out of their ports. In 1394, a fleet consisting of 35 warships and 3000 men failed to dispatch Störtebeker and his allies, but the "Victuallers," were finally defeated in 1401 by a Hanseatic fleet. Störtebeker was beheaded after being caught alive near Hamburg. Störtebeker who drank a stout "beaker at a gulp" was actually a ruthless murderer but was revered as a hero in a drama performed in communist East Germany during the Cold War, postdating World War II. The Communist writers and dramatists of East Germany elevated Störtebeker to a seaborne Robin Hood who robbed from rich merchants of the Hanseatic League and gave to the poor.[55]

Gerhard Ohling, a 20th-century genealogist in Aurich, Ostfriesland, citing a late 18th century lexicographer of Aurich,[56] proposed another interpretation of *Wykhof* based upon an Indo-European word root nearly identical in form to *weik but connoting a holy or consecrated place. In combination with *-hof*, the compound meaning would denote a sacred space, or sanctuary.[57] The reconstructed PIE (proto Indo-European) *weik has several homonyms or near homonyms. Those forms reflected in English *wick* or *wic* as in the words: candlewick, wicked, wicker (basket), and in victim will not concern us

---

[55] Well illustrated outdoor and indoor drama performances and exhibits featuring the popular story of Störtebeker are included in *Störtebeker: Dichtung und Wahrheit* by Harm Bents, Bernd Flessner, and Marin Stromann (Verlag SoltauKurier, 2003). Very useful historical commentary by Harm Bents is provided on the literature and imagery of the folk hero over several centuries.

[56] Ohling probably utilized the *Altfriesisches Wörterbuch* of Tilemann Dothias Wiarda (Aurich 1786). Because Ohling's interpretation of Wykhof may not be justified, does not mean that all his contributions should be doubted. Evidently, much of his work is worthy of our consideration.

[57] Short monosyllabic words composed of only one vowel and one or two consonants are very frequently homonymous. Common examples of homonyms in English are: *deer* and *dear*. pea and pee; gait and gate; red and read; weight and wait.

here, but the nearly homonymous PIE *weih/weik as in Weihnachten has to be considered as a possible origin of *wik* in Wykhof because of the peculiar histories of Marienhafe, Klein Borsum, and three other settlements within the surrounding Brookmerland area. The reconstructed *weik/weih is supported by data from Gothic and Old High German *weih* 'holy', and Old Frisian *weik* 'separate;' *wia* 'consecrate;' *withe* 'relics;' and *wilinge* 'sorcery.' [58] Normally, the space around a church would be termed *kerkhof* or *kirchhof*. Ohling interprets the term *wyk* + *hof* as referring to churchyards in four locations. Under the entry for *wik*, in the *Altfriesisches Wörterbuch* (1840) compiled by Karl von Richthofen,[59] "Maria howe et Utengra howe et Victoris howe, et Aurec howe" (Marienhafe, Engerhafe, Victorbur, and Aurich) were all kirchhöfen regarded as sacred enclosures. Each *howe* was regarded as the "Weichbild der Stadt." As evidence for a special defensive sanctuary, Ohling noted the former wall enclosing the market, the tower at Marienhafe, and historical legal protections associated with church buildings and properties at Marienhafe and the three other sites. Ohling speculated that the earliest converts to Christianity at Wykhof hosted representatives of the Bishop from Münster before the church was erected, ca. 1250 AD[60]

---

[58] Walter Baetke, *Das Heilige in Germanischen*. (Tübingen 1942): 80-90.

[59] Dr. Karl Freiherr von Richthofen, *Altfriesisches Wörterbuch*, (Göttingen 1840).

[60] Owners or inhabitants of a Frisian estate hosting Christians could have been controversial. Ost Frisia was the last area of continental Europe to be converted to Christianity. St. Boniface who introduced Christianity to Germany is celebrated every year by both Lutherans and Catholics in Germany, but he was killed on 5 June 754 when he attempted to proselytize in pagan Friesland. The Frisian heathens, who occupied the moors near the southern coast of the North Sea, earned their reputation, beginning with the Romans, for being fiercely independent. "Eala frya Fresena!" (Hail, free Frisians). Freemen met in general assemblies. Medieval serfdom never developed in Friesland to the extent it did elsewhere in Europe. Many Dutch students and other refugees who protested or resisted Nazi persecution in the 1930s and 1940s were hidden, and often assisted by Frisians as the victims of the Hitler regime were attempting to escape across the North Sea. (My friend and colleague, Ari van Tienhoven, the endocrinologist now retired from Cornell, was among those Dutch students hidden by Frisian farmers during World War II).

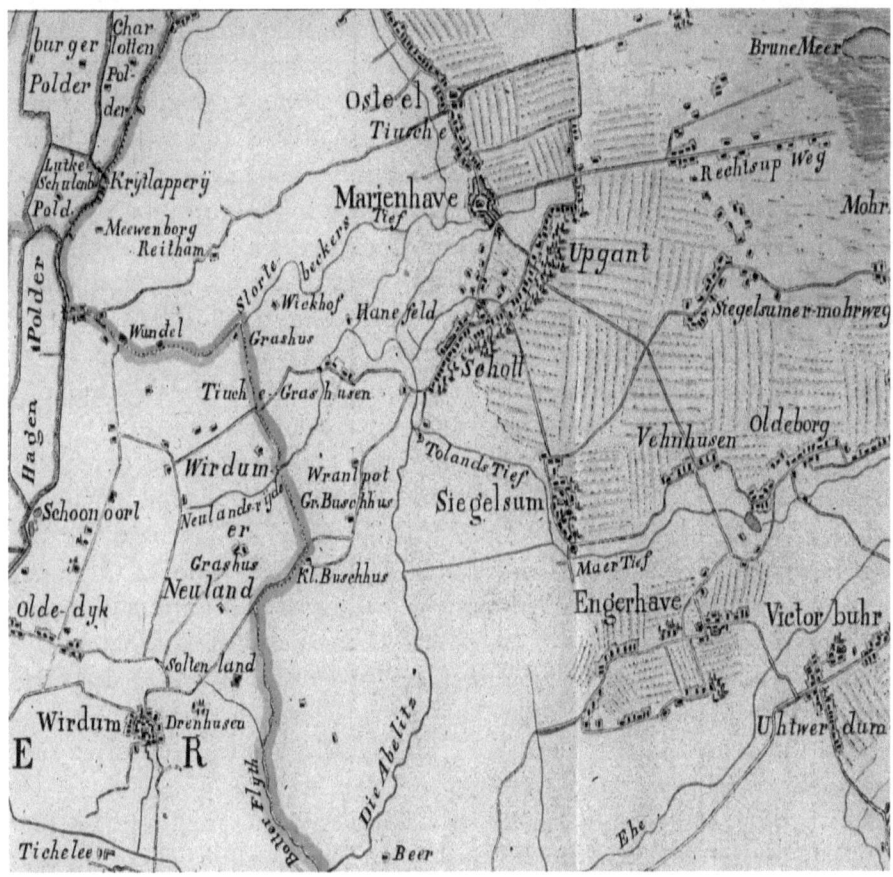

Figure 8. Marienhafe area excerpted from a hand drawn map of Ostfriesland and Harlingerland, ca. 1800.[61]   Three communities with a Wik/markt that were referred to by Ohling can be seen on this map. Engerhafe and Victor buhr can be seen to the southeast of Marienhafe. Evidently all had an outdoor market adjacent to a church. This map also shows the position of Wiekhof just a half mile southwest of Marienhafe on the south side of Störtebeker Tief.

---

[61]   „Neue geographische Special Charte von dem Furstenthum Ostfries und dem Harrlingerland- Aufgenommen und bearbeitet in den Jahren 1798 bis 1802 durch den vormaligen Holländischen Artillerie Capitain W. Camp und dessen beide Gehulfen, die vormaligen Holländischen Artillerie Lieutenants H. Bunnik und W. van der Linden." Die handgezeichnete Original-Karte aus dem Jahr 1806 ist im Besitz der Staatsbibliothek zu Berlin - Preußischer Kulturbesitz – (Signatur Kart. N 27.299). Copy provided by Harm Bents.

Wykhof, interpreted as an enclosed sacred space around the church raises immediate questions about its specific temporal and spatial application in this vicinity. It seems unlikely that both the house-barn on Stortebeker Tief and the walled-in settlement around the church would both be named Wykhof at the same time. Could the reference have been to the larger area including both the household estate and the enclosed church property? Was the *Wykhof* term in use at the house-barn before the church was built? The first written documents referring to this area were written in medieval Latin. Did the clerics accurately perceive and describe local language terminology? Did they tranlate *wik* as *vicus?* Evidently, a privately owned estate called *Marienhof* was given to an order of monks to build the church. This would imply that two separate terms were applied to the Wykhof estate and the Marienhof estate. The dates for establishing usage priorities here are difficult to determine without ample relevant chronological records, but the evidence gathered, so far, does not bode well for the theory of Gerhard Ohling. The religious connotation of Wykhof does not appear in early documents relating to the house-barn or to Marienhafe. The question is not whether Ohling's theory is logical. The question is whether his meaning was ever current in the local dialect. If *Wykhoff* was also commonly used at Utengra howe, et Victoris howe, et Aurec howe, how good is the evidence? If it was used, did it connote a sacred place or a settlement on a bay or waterway?

Ohling's interpretation seems slightly more justified for a second Wykhoff estate near Borsum (in the vicinity of Emden) where there is good evidence that the estate was the locus of early proselytizing activities of the Catholic church. (Ohling's own ancestors evidently had connections to The Wykhoff of Klein Borsum). The property was first referred to as Langen Kloster, or Jakobskloster because the cloister was dedicated to the biblical Jacob. (The middle name of our family historian Wilhelm J. Wykhoff is Jacob.) The property was once a nunnery. In 1288, the population was 160 but the estate was later flooded and finally abandoned by the church. The later house and barn structure (Fig. 9 below) came to be referred to as The Wykoff although tenant families who lived there did not utilize the surname until the 17th century.[62] But if Wykhoff owes its meaning to a sacred enclosure, why was it not used earlier at Klein Borsum? A pretentious coat of arms was eventually created which was associated with a later Wykhoff resident family at Klein Borsum, but this is hardly evidence for medieval knighthood.

---

[62] Wilhelm J. Wykhoff, 2008, pp. 17-18.

Because of its early association with a cloister, Gerhard Ohling may have over generalized his sacred interpretation of *wik* from The Wykhoff II, at Klein Borsum and Aurich to its occurrence at Marienhafe. Ohling resided in Aurich, which was founded in medieval times for the purpose of trading, and where a church, Lambertikirche with extensive property, was placed next to the Wik/Markt.[63] This historical convergence of

Figure 9. The Wykhoff near Klein Borsum. 1980 photograph from Wilhelm J. Wykhoff, *Die Geschichte der Familie Wykhoff*, 2008, p. 26. Parts of this structure date from the 16th or 17th century. The house and barn were occupied by descendants of the Wykhoff family from the 1600s until 1922. Jan Jacobs Wykhoff was the son of Jacob Janssen and the first to use the surname at The Wykhoff near Klein Borsum in the 1660s. Although the bricks were crumbling, the structure was not demolished until 1999. The structure was barely above the water table and was surrounded by ditches, except for a driveway that led to the road named Wykhoffweg.

---

[63]   These spatial relationships can be seen on a map of medieval Aurich (ca. 1250 AD) reconstructed by G. Kronsweide in a 2009 festschrift for Dr. Waldemar Reinhart. *Nachrichten des Marschenrates zur Förderung der Forschung im Küstengebiet der Nordsee,* Heft 46 / 2009, p. 58. I am indebted to Kay Blaas for providing me a digital copy.

market and church properties led Ohling to believe that this was the origin of Wykhof, but all indications are that the secular market in Aurich preceded the medieval church. Of course, the reconstructed Indo-Germanic word roots for *wik*- and *–hof,* predate Christianity by several millennia. My interpretation is that neither The Wykhof near Marienhafe nor The Wykhof near Borsum were ever a *Weichbild* or sacred center of a town. They had secular origins even if they later hosted visiting Bishops.

Ohling also opined that there was a genetic connection between The Wykhoff in Upgant-Schott and The Wykoff in Klein Borsum, but the evidence, so far, seems only circumstantial and inadequate. The Wykhof near Marienhafe was built on the property of the Chieftain Ter Braeck and it was the oldest structure on the Brookmer land reclaimed from the sea by dikes.[64] Although the origins and histories of the settlements and the tenant families of the two Wykhofs at Marienhafe and Borsum are nearly simultaneous, and somewhat parallel, I am not aware of any direct connection noted in the *Emder Jahrbuch*. What both have in common is that they were settlements near Ems River bays, and associated canals.

Harm Bents has recently referred me to legal documents, ca. 1276 AD, in which the Wik at Marienhafe is clearly identified as the Marktgebiet (marketplace).[65] There is no association mentioned to the church or sacred space even though Catholocism was well established here by this time. Perhaps more telling than the negative evidence, i.e., the absence of the religious interpretation of Wykhof in early glossaries, is a 1956 communication from Andreas Baumann to Gerhard Ohling: "'Wykhof' sehe ich so. Der Name kommt wohl von 'wik' dem Marktplatz zu Marienhafe. Dass W. [wik] mal zur Kirch gehört hat, glaube ich nicht."[66] Obviously, Baumann believed that the correct interpretation was the secular one and not the sacred meaning promulgated by Ohling. It seems only fitting that the economic rather than the religious interpretation is supported in early documents; the Greek *woikos* or *oikos* derives from PIE *weik and forms the basis for our modern English word *economics*. Of course, the compound word *Wykhof* was first scripted much later in Northern Germanic scripts and

---

[64] Holtmanns writing in the *Emder Jahrbuch*, Band 7, Seite 166.

[65] Wybren Jan Buma, *Die Brokmer Rechtshandschriften*, `s-Gravenhage 1949, S. 45 – 48 und 301, 302. Original documents archived in Oldenburg and Hannover.

[66] Excerpt from letter of Andreas Baumann communicated to me by Harm Bents. June 2013.

has its own secular history from an extended household in Indo Germanic to settlement on a bay in Northern Germanic.

The Christian interpretation of Wykhof is not supported by hard evidence. If the house-barn had survived, dendrochronology could have been employed to compare the rings in its beams with those in beams of the Marienhafe church. Perhaps some answers from stratified sediments, if ever analyzed by future archaeologists, can describe the purpose of any earlier structures on the two sites that might help determine the local priority of meanings for *wik* and *Wykhof*. There is already evidence from an excavation that a wooden church was constructed as early as the ninth century on the site where Marienkirche was built around 1250 AD[67] but no document has been found from that early time that applies *wik* to any sacred space here. (Large Christian churches built of durable quarried stone came to Ostfriesland much later than to West Friesland). Any occupied site predating the acceptance of Christianity by Frisians would only be a sacred space or a sanctuary if it could be shown by archaeological evidence to be associated with pagan practices.

The traditional Northern Germanic meaning of *wik* as a settlement on the high ground where settlers establish a permanent square for trading is descriptive and seems appropriate for Marienhafe, Utengra, Victoris, and Aurec; yet none of these locales adopted Wykhof as its permanent place name. As Christianity swept across Europe in medieval times, nobles and bishops built churches, but this is a matter of circumstance and does not require that the meaning of Wykhof be expanded to connote sacredness wherever these circumstances converge. The wide distribution of *wik* meaning a household or settlement on a bay throughout the North Germanic language area predates the introduction of Christianity and provides a compelling argument in favor of the secular interpretation for origins. That does not mean that later connotations or meaning shifts in local settings are to be excluded. Dialectal variations in meaning are to be expected over time.

After AD 1400, the time of Störtebeker, the unique additional connotation for the term *Wykhof* as a place of refuge begins to be listed among its meanings in glossaries and dictionaries of Ost Frisian. If and how this meaning was extended into the dialects of West and North Frisian speakers remains to be investigated historically. The Wykhoff at Klein Borsum does not seem to have been such a place of refuge.

---

[67]   Johann Gerhard Schomerus, *Die Marienkirche von Marienhafe*. 1986. Norden: Verlag Soltau-Kurier, pp. 10-11.

Dialectology reached a high level of development in 19th century Europe. Dialect atlases were published which were based on solid empirical research. A dialect walk could be taken from Belgium through France, Switzerland, Provencal into Spain, or Italy. Along the way, people could understand each other in neighboring villages, but Belgian French could not be understood in Spain or Italy, because of shifts in word meaning and pronunciations. When speakers of a large community no longer understand a majority of utterances spoken by members of another community, we say they are speaking different languages. In the abstract, we can distinguish language, dialect, and idiolect. Some of the earliest dictionaries of Frisian were compiled or edited by a single literate, erudite author. Perhaps the lexicon of Tilemann Wiarda, which was utilized by Gerhard Ohling, fits into this category of dictionaries based on the author's idiolect. Modern dictionaries are typically based on surveys of speakers along with textual and statistical analyses of published works, i.e., they are based on the language and dialects of whole communities, not on the idiolect of a single lexicographer. Early dictionaries are extremely useful since they are often all we have to represent the meaning of a word at a particular time and place, but how representative the given meaning is for the whole linguistic community may be questioned. Dictionary entries in the OED *(Oxford English Dictionary)* typically have multiple meanings listed; some more archaic, esoteric, or localized than others. Usages of some meanings are simply abandoned and lost. However, it is important to recognize that some meanings are invalid even if they are accepted by many speakers and often repeated.

The criteria for an acceptable meaning stipulates that it must not only be shared by members of a language community, but that it be correct or true. Thus, if the meaning of asparagus is said to derive from "sparrow" + "grass," the proposition must be determined by its actual history. If one searched only documents in English from the 17th century until the comparative method of linguistics was established early in the 19th century, one would be tempted to accept the folk etymology as true. The truth is that the word was known to ancient speakers of Latin and Greek, and most likely derived from the parent PIE root *sp(h)er(e)g- "to spring up." If one looks for the history of the compound *wyck* + *hof,* only in Dutch, it will not even be found. It will be found in Swedish and Frisian. Unfortunately, the false etymology for Wyckoff is the one that is most frequently encountered in the literature of 20th-century America and now on internet. It has been accepted by many, but it is false. The surname actually came from Friesland and was not created in America. Whether the immediate proximal meaning was a household, or settlement on a bay or waterway, or a place of refuge, it was surely not located in the Netherlands, but in Friesland where it was usually written Wyk- (not Wijc-, Wijk, or Wyck-). As all types of evidence indicate, the name *Wykhof*, no matter how it is spelled or how it is interpreted, is Frisian rather than Dutch. The fabricated meaning of *Wijk* + *hof* being a Dutch word interpreted as a "town clerk" was neither an established meaning in any speech community nor a correct and true meaning.

In Dutch, *gemeente* translates as town; a town clerk is a *gemeente secretaris*. A town dweller is a *stedsemeer* and towns folk are *stedelingen*. A village is a *dorp,* and a villager is a *dorpeling*. A settlement is a *nederzetting,* and a settler who moves onto drained land is a *kolonist*. These Dutch words are cognate to, or borrowed from, those commonly used in German. As in Latin *vicus,* the Dutch meaning of *wijk* usually applies to a district of a larger urban area, rather than to an original settlement. A Dutch inhabitant of such a district is a *wijkbewohner*. A person living on a bay is a *baiibewoner*. In Old Norse and Icelandic, the corresponding word was *vikingr*, derivable more directly from the reconstructed PIE (proto Indo-European) root *weik.

Unfortunately, the current CD version of *The Wyckoff Family in America* records Pieter Claessen as born in the Netherlands, with Claes Cornelisze as the father and Margaret van der Goes as the mother. For this, there is absolutely no evidence. Perhaps because Pieter Claessen sailed on a Dutch boat and was indentured to serve in a Dutch colony, it was just assumed with no documentation, even by editors of genealogy publications, that "Pieter Claesen Wyckoff, the common ancestor of the Wyckoff family in this country, emigrated from Netherlands..."[68]   It is also disappointing to read the recent (1995) comment of a professional genealogist associated with *The New York Genealogical and Biographical Record (NYGBR),* "...some names, such as Wyckoff, seem to have no relationship to what is known of the family."[69] Yet, the Wykhof estate south of Norden in Ostfriesland undoubtedly figured prominently in the choice of a surname by Pieter Claessen.

---

[68]   Quoted from *New York Biographical and Genealogical Record* 12.4 (Oct 1881): 153.

[69]   Kenn Stryker-Rodda, "New Netherland Naming Systems and Customs," *New York Biographical and Genealogical Record* 126, #1 (1995): 35-45.

Helen Wikoff and Bernhard Hall of the American Wyckoff Association visited the Ost Frisian site in 1983. A "Home to Holland" tour, organized by members of the Wyckoff Association, travelled to Germany in 1987 to visit the Wykhof estate. The occupant living on the property then, H. Arends, courteously greeted 48 American Wyckoffs, their friends, and local dignitaries. The bay and waterway to the west are now farmland reclaimed by colonists (see Fig. 4, p. 22). For the relative locations of The Wykhof and Marienhafe, as mapped ca. 1800, see Fig. 8, p. 39. To locate the road going by the site of the former estate on a Google map, simply zoom in on: Hanefeld-Wykhof, Upgant-Schott, Germany. There is a small museum in the Marienhafe church tower featuring the life of Störtebeker, and the view of the surrounding flat terrain from this tower, or what was left of it after 1829, is reputedly something to behold.

240. CANAL WITH COTTAGES AND A BOAT

Figure 10. Etching by unknown artist, ca. 1640-1650. Reproduced from *The Complete Etchings of Rembrandt*, edited by Bruce & Seena Harris. Crown Publishers, 1970.

Notes on Wyckoff Documentary History

While *The Wyckoff Family in America* is a very useful genealogy for American descendants of Pieter Claessen, the introductory chapter should never have been published without being authenticated. The story regarding the origin of the surname is uninformed conjecture. The erroneous, but deliberately deceptive genealogy of Wyckoff progenitors in Europe originated with a manuscript submitted by Gustave Anjou who had been commissioned by William F. Wyckoff. (See account in *Wyckoff Bulletin*, December 1945). Unfortunately, Gustave Anjou (as a simple Google search shows) was a classic, fraudulent, self-professed genealogist who exacted high fees for lengthy and detailed pedigrees which typically linked American *nouveau riche* to existing genealogies of European royalty, and nobility with coats of arms. Under the entry for Gustave Anjou in the online *Encyclopedia of Genealogy,* it is noted "Any information taken from his works should be scrutinized with greater-than-usual care, and every asserted fact verified." The Wyckoff family is publicly listed on internet among more than 300 victims of Dr. Anjou (http://personal.linkline.com/xymox/fraud/anjousbu.htm).

It is to the credit of several leading genealogists, including Donald Lines Jacobus and George E. McCracken, that some of the forgeries of Gustave Anjou have been exposed. In fact, a contemporary of Anjou and competent genealogist, J. Gardner Bartlett, had set forth the evidence to show that the Higgins pedigree published (1916) in *The New York Genealogical and Biographical Record* was false.[70] Unfortunately, the NYGBR editor, John Totten, defended the author of the pedigree, saying that it had been verified by a genealogist, but did not say that the genealogist was Gustave Anjou.[71] It seems that editors can be positively impressed by the credentials of the author or by masses of properly documented citations as they accept or reject articles. As Robert Charles Anderson, the noted genealogist, wrote in the recent (1991)

---

[70] Robert Charles Anderson, "We Wuz Robbed, The 'modus operandi' of Gustave Anjou," *Genealogical Journal,* 1991: 50.

Orra Eugene Monnette, "Richard Higgins of Plymouth and Eastham, Mass., and Piscataway, N.J., and Some of His Descendants," *The New York Genealogical and Biographical Record* 46 (October 1916): 387-394: 47 (January 1916): 20-32.

[71] "Corrections and Additions to Published Genealogical Works," *The New York Genealogical and Biographical Record* 57 (July 1926): 298-299.

article, "We Wuz Robbed! The *modus operandi* of Gustave Anjou," "...An unfortunate feature of Anjou's work is that even in the enlightened era in which we live, there are still many who are blinded by the volume of genuine records supplied by Anjou, and swallow along with these records the few fabricated items that make the pedigree as a whole worthless."[72] If a single link is false, the entire chain of descent is false. Among the examples cited by Anderson, is a 1987 reprint of a 1919 report on the Shapleigh family by Gustave Anjou. The recent reprint is adorned with a lengthy Foreword commending Anjou for his diligent efforts and his doctorate. But even the degree was faked as was proved by Gordon L. Remington in "Gustave, We Hardly Knew Ye: A Portrait of Herr Anjou as a Jungberg."[73] There is no record of Gustaf Ludvig Ljungberg or anyone with any of his pseudonyms attending Uppsala University in his native Sweden as he claimed. Sometime after serving 6 months at hard labor in the Västeros County prison (1886-1887) for forgery, he changed his name. His trail is picked up again in 1900 when he was listed as a genealogist in the *New York Genealogical Biographical Record* as Gustave Anjou.[74] He had migrated to New York, assumed his wife's maiden surname, and launched a new career.

Upon opening the file which is the current (2012) CD version of *The Wyckoff Family in America,* the first page shows Pieter Claesen Wyckoff, as the son of Claes Cornelisze and Margaret van der Goes, born in the Netherlands on 6 January 1625 (which, as noted above, would have him 11 years old when he contracted to be an indentured laborer in the Rensselaerswyck colony). It is far more likely that Pieter's age was closer to 20 than to 10 when he contracted to work at a man's wage. This false link to a birth in Sweden or Netherlands is obviously the keystone to Anjou's story of royal blood running in the veins of Pieter Claesen and his American descendants. The digitized ghost of the ignoble Gustave Anjou lives on in the Wyckoff House Association in spite of all the evidence that he was a professional forger of hundreds of pedigrees. It is sad to contemplate that one hundred years ago, wealthy Americans were willing to pay as much as $9000 to Anjou for detailed genealogies, but what is even more disheartening is to see so many of his fake pedigrees still regarded as true family lineages. Although Anjou

---

[72]   Anderson,(1991): 50. Anjou was not the only fraudulent genealogist in his time; neither was he the last. The late Louis P. de Boer specialized in concocting European ancestries for many early Dutch colonists.

[73]   Gordon L. Remington, "Gustave We Hardly Knew Ye: A Portrait of Herr Anjou as a Jungberg," *Genealogical Journal*, 1991: 64-65.

[74]   Remington (1991): 66-67.

authored several genealogies, much of his extensive work was incorporated in family histories and books written by others which makes it difficult for honest researchers to recognize. Anjou skillfully cited an overwhelming number of documents that actually exist, but then spliced in false connections that he knew would please his clients. Anjou gave them what they wanted. He had been convicted of forgery in his native Sweden but was able to make it a lucrative vocation in America. Those of us doing fastidious genealogy are perhaps overly impressed by proper citations to documents. Anjou overwhelmed his clients with citations to actual documents and some of the information was factual, but the utility of obsessive documentation must be questioned. To follow up on each and every document cited to discover now which links are fictional would be difficult. It is imperative that a genealogist, or editor of genealogical works acquire an adequate historical background to distinguish between true and false lineages. The actual relevant documentation is a necessary starting point but if the truth be known, it will come in the quality of the interpretation. The persistent search for truth is ultimately more important than the fact finding. Which facts are selected and how they are interpreted is crucial. Unfortunately in genealogy, gaps are often filled in by imaginative story-telling with too little devotion to truth seeking. Facts, as well as their connections, are too easily fabricated and too often repeated. False beliefs (such as Pieter Claessen being Dutch) come to be accepted as true when they are repeated frequently and authoritatively, a pattern we know so well from Nazi propaganda. As Ernest Flagg, a well-known genealogist comments, many people suppose a statement to be true if it is old enough, "…but one who examines critically, soon comes to the conclusion that in genealogy, at least, the art of lying has made little progress through the ages."[75] The indomitable entrepreneurial spirit continues to flourish in the industry of family history.[76]

---

[75] Ernest Flagg quoted in *Genealogical Evidence* by Noel C. Stevenson. (Aegean Park Press, 1989): 30.

[76] Amazon.com offers *The Wyckoff Name in History*, one of nearly 300,000 titles available in their *Our Name in History* series, which are booklets assembled from stock phrases about immigration history and genealogy from Ancestry.com. The information about origins and meanings of surnames is typically inaccurate. We are told that this book has "89 clean pages, with many illustrations, a glossary of family history terms, and a list of sources, as well as pedigree chart and family group sheets. An overview of the occurrence of the Wyckoff family name in the census, military records, immigration records, and

The Old World Progenitors of the Wyckoff Family (edited and published by William L Wyckoff, 1936) is a case in point for selecting among facts and falsely linking them to other unrelated facts to tell a story. To have Pieter Claessen born 1625 in Middleburg, p. 21, (or at Böda on the Swedish island of Öland, p.49) descended from Eric, one of the early chieftains or kings of Sweden, ca. 800 AD through King Harald of England and Claes Cornelisze in the Netherlands is not a credible narrative to a historian. A significant portion of the earliest emigrants to America had no surname and no known lineage. In Europe, they were still immersed in a feudalistic society and condemned to a servile existence by the low status of their birth, landless-ness, and severe marriage restrictions. Illegitimacy was the norm. Many of the single male emigrants never knew their biological father. If we are to see the forest, and not just a family tree, then history trumps genealogy. It is necessary to search out and utilize whatever written records exist, but we must also be willing to accept the fact that there was never any documentation for many lineages, especially in the times before surnames became mandatory for whole populations. Unfortunately, the European genealogy of the Wyckoff family in America still bears the earmarks of Gustave Anjou.[77] However, the surname meaning

---

much more, along with some introductory information on genealogical research and time lines in history." Sound good? The sentence differs from those found in all the others in the series only by the substitution of the name and a slight tweaking in the number of pages. The author of these books (all dated 2007) is "Ancestry" (an interesting pseudonym for a computer?) and the publisher: Generations Network of Provo, Utah. 28 out of 32 customer reviewers on Amazon.com gave the minimum 1 out of 5 star rating for the *Our Name in History* series, castigating Amazon.com and Ancestry.com for charging a minimum of $20 for so much useless generic information. Ancestry does insert a disclaimer that data should not be confused with fact! Of course, these computer-generated booklets never go out of print. Also at ancestry.com, under the heading of "All Public Member Photos & Scanned Documents results for Wyckoff," one can view the colored flags of Sweden and Netherlands, two different coats of arms for Wyckoff, and even one for Van Shouen.

[77] To the credit of Herbert J. Wyckoff who wrote Chapter I in the 1950 edition of *The Wyckoff Family in America*, he penned an understatement regarding the inclusive report of Dr. Anjou, "...few will accept it *in toto* as more than a fantastic possibility; certainly not as a water-tight law of descent of a single family" (p. 1).

propagated in Old World Progenitors and disseminated by the Wyckoff Association of America, was evidently contributed not by Anjou, but by William F. Wyckoff and his editors.

In the second (1950) edition of the *Wyckoff Family in America*, William Forman Wyckoff opined, "Pieter Claesen had been a local judge and the name came from this fact, the 'Wyk' meaning a parish and 'hof' meaning a court. Thus the name would mean Pieter Claesen of the town court." If *Wijk* was listed as a 'parish' in a dictionary, the dictionary has not yet been found. If *hof* was listed as a judicial court, it would be unusual. A.J.F. van Laer, the expert in 17th-century Dutch had written many years earlier, "the word *hof* is never used in connection with the lower court, and the combination *wijk-hof* is entirely unknown in old or modern Dutch in the sense of a town court."[78] According to the authors of *Old World Progenitors*, "...at the very outset we are confronted by the fact that nowhere in the Old World does the name Wyckoff appear" (p.11). "Wijkhof, or Wyckoff, is not an Old World surname, but a derivative adopted in this country by Pieter Claesen, a magistrate of the town of Flatlands under the Dutch government" (p. 41). Here we are given a gratuitous translation of Pieter Claesen Wyckoff as "Pieter Claesen of the Town Court" by the author (pp 12-13). In retrospect, it is hilarious to read that spelling variations of the name "...are traceable to current lack of education and consequent indifference to exactness" (p. 13). Apparently, the ahistorical author and family genealogist was a nominalist who believed that he had arrived at the one and only true spelling and true meaning of the surname. Finding no Wyckoff surname in the Netherlands, William Forman Wyckoff supposed that the surname Wyckoff was an invention made in America. He ignored the ample evidence that Pieter Claessen came from Norden, now within Germany; and he made no honest effort to investigate the possibility of a Wykhof place name and subsequent surname in modern Germany.

Neither the story of the well-intentioned William F. Wyckoff nor that of the fraudulent Gustave Anjou can stand the scientific test of the pragmaticist maxim that the truth of a statement can only be determined by its ultimate consequences. The consequences of following either of these two fictions about the origins and meaning of Wyckoff can only lead to dead ends.

---

[78] Hoppin (1932): 125.

Dead ends, contradictions, and confusion are now reigning on dozens of websites designed to exploit the fantastic demand of amateur genealogists for do-it-yourself construction of family trees. Many give no source for their data and interpretations, but when sources are cited, the publications of family associations are often utilized. And even when they are not cited, the familiar source can easily be inferred.

Under the entry for Wyckoff on wikipedia.com (last modified on 19 March 2013) it is stated regarding the selection of the surname by Pieter Claessen, "Most commonly accepted is that he chose this name from the Dutch words 'Wyk' meaning parish and 'hof' meaning court. There are Dutch Wyckoffs as well, leading to speculation that there may have been some old world association." The Wikipedia author actually embellishes the original source by claiming that there are Dutch Wyckoffs, in contradiction to the original claim that the name was invented in America. The freewheeling liberty of the internet is in countless cases encouraging creative story-telling at the expense of truth seeking.

On FamilyTreeMaker.com (June 2013), it is stated: "Pieter Claesen Wyckoff was born January 06, 1624/25 in Boda, Oland Island, Netherlands." The author has conflated the two contradictory places of birth listed in *The Old World Progenitors of the Wyckoff Family*, not realizing that Boda is nowhere near the Netherlands. The invented meaning that "parish" + "town court" = Wyckoff is repeated from the 1950 *Wyckoff Family in America*. It is further stated that the original spelling of the name was Wijckhoff and that the nearest approach to that is Wyckoff. Among the thousands of profiles that include Pieter Claessen in their family tree on ancestry.com, nearly half list Sweden and the other half list Netherlands as his place of birth.

At Geni.com, the two contradictory places of birth are also repeated and combined. Pieter Claesen is said to have been born on 6 January 1625 at Boda, Oland Island, Netherlands. On the same page, it is stated that he was born in Sweden, and that his father's surname was Van Schoewen. As the son of Claes Cornelissen Van Schouw and Margaret van der Goes, Pieter Claessen would have had about 9 siblings in his immediate family plus 11 half siblings by his father's other wife; and now their thousands of descendants can potentially be added to the Wyckoff family tree on Geni.com with van Schouw included among other leading surnames such as: Clawson, Classen, Van Schouen, Van der Goes, Cos, Corneliszen, and Cornelisen. Geni.com, was launched in 2007 as Wikigenia, a social networking and genealogy website, with the aim of creating one single World Family Tree. There was no fee for adding family trees without any verification. The Los Angeles based Geni.com developed a collaborative online family tree editor that went viral. A user base of 7 million registered users, mostly Americans, was quickly generated with over 135 million profiles contributed. Just one giant Geni.com tree grows at the rate of 2 million profiles per month. Members of families are "ranked" by the number of contributions they make to a family tree. Perpetrators of unverified linkages are being rewarded. There are no rewards for disconnecting unverified links, which would contract the World Family Tree. It would seem appropriate if Gustave Anjou were to be given a grand prize, *in memoriam*, for his contribution to the growing Wyckoff family tree on Geni.com. Through expedient internet media, false information about Wyckoff genealogy is now being multiplied exponentially. Amateur genealogy is exploding on the world wide web. Of course, there is much overlap in the family trees between websites. In fact, the same family tree may occur several times even on a single website. Even if the many duplications could be identified or eliminated, the numbers for profiles and family trees would still be staggering.

The problem now is not so much one of a few fraudulent professional genealogists, but of hundreds of uninformed amateurs and genealogy website managers who are not only proliferating oft-repeated falsehoods but are also creating false links online *ad nauseum*. I recently counted over 51 genealogy websites by googling on internet. Online do-it-yourself genealogy is obviously a multimillion dollar industry. Werelate.org has wiki pages for 700,000 families or over 2 million persons. FamilySearch, developed by the Mormon church lists over 60 million people in the Pedigree Resource File. GenCircles.com offers a surname search among 90 million ancestors. The World Family Tree at Genealogy.com covers 130 million names in 180,000 trees. MyTrees.com has over 200 million names from family group sheets and contributed family trees. WorldConnect, part of the RootsWeb project is supported by Ancestry.com. Ancestry.com has 800,000 paying subscribers, 14 million registered users. User-contributed entries approach 700 million people. The majority of sites charge a monthly or annual fee for detailed information. Tree submissions are usually free, but annual membership fees are typically charged for access to a lot of unverified data. World Wide Web genealogy has become big business. Over $10 million was contributed to Geni.com by private venture capital firms. Now the older and larger MyHeritage genealogy dotcom has bought Geni.com for an undisclosed amount. MyHeritage has about 1.35 billion profiles on their international website. It was on the MyHeritage website that Klaus Beyer's German family tree was automatically linked to my own maternal line because of our common ancestor, Felicitas Sammetinger. In our case, there is enough agreement with documented names and dates to verify links to a common ancestor, but how are false links to be identified and eliminated? With no one to verify linkages, family trees have grown into works of fictive national forests. Family associations and national genealogical associations have been relegated to the periphery.

Conclusions

By going beyond the known origins of Pieter Claessen and focussing on the history and meaning of Wyckoff, we have been able to prove that the surname is Frisian, not Dutch. We have been able to explain why many Wyckoffs in America are unable to trace their ancestor to Pieter Claessen. We have been able to demonstrate that the meaning of *Wyk* in Northern Germanic is different from the meaning of *Wijk* in Dutch. The Wykhof near Marienhafe and The Wykhof near Borsum conform to the meaning of the surname as a settlement near a bay, or with a water transport connection to a bay. The significance of this linguistic approach is that it casts a wider net over space and time, providing real world contexts for determining meanings of the surname in actual speech communities. While DNA testing can invalidate a falsified birth certificate and trace specific ancestral traits over millions of years, linguistic methodology can still provide much valuable data from the prehistoric Neolithic to the historic Medieval and Modern periods. The fact that the Wykhoff surname is common in modern telephone books from Lower Saxony (including Ostfriesland) but nothing comparable appears in Dutch telephone books makes sense if one knows the history of the name. The Wyckoff Association of America would do well to establish a working relationship with the Wykhoff Association of Germany. Wyckoff immigrants from Germany should be solicited for membership in the American association. DNA testing, news of reunions, and educational travel between America and Ostfriesland, should be encouraged by both family associations.

Among the sources for Wyckoff ancestry during the 20th century, the publications of the Wyckoff Family Association did not serve well as guides for Wyckoff family members searching for truth, particularly with regard to our European progenitors, and the origins and meaning of the surname. In fact, the misinformation led many of us away from the primary sources and their competent commentators, especially Arnold Johan Ferdinand van Laer, New York State Archivist, and translator of the voluminous Rensselaerswyck manuscripts, who was thoroughly familiar with 17th century Dutch language and culture. Following him, and also cited in the passages above, Charles A. Hoppin, William J. Hoffman, Richard Schemerhoorn, Morton Wagman, David S. Cohen, Hans Schrader, and Wilhelm Wykhoff made worthy contributions which emphasized the Norden, Ostfriesland origin, and directly contradicted information propagated and mailed to members of the Wyckoff Association.[79]

Hopefully, what is now known about the history and meanings of the surname will discourage further dissemination of false lineages and fictional accounts of Wyckoff family history. It is genuinely disquieting to open the current CD edition of *The Wyckoff Family in America* only to see the first entry listing Claes Corneliszen as the father of our progenitor Pieter Wyckoff. The repetition of fraudulent genealogical information is a disservice to the family and to honest researchers past and present.

Family associations, especially those like the Wyckoff Association which had previously established long-term genealogy projects including publications, are being urged to step up to their responsibility to disprove false information and to offer a superior verification process for establishing links while approving new members for inclusion in the family tree. Family trees for American Wyckoffs not directly descended from Pieter Claessen should also be launched for future reference and possible genetic relationships to common Ostfrisian ancestors.

For the Wyckoff Association, it means that they first must promulgate the detailed information to disprove the false links so entrenched in the literature. Both amateur and professional genealogists demand specific evidence. This contribution to the History and Meaning of Wyckoff was intended to serve that purpose.

Secondly, the Wyckoff Association must acknowledge that much of the false information was disseminated by the Association itself, and

---

[79] I am probably not the only American descendant of Pieter Claessen who travelled through Amsterdam and Hannover more than once before 1974, unaware that the ancestral Wykhof estate was still in existence near Norden in East Friesland. At the time, I had read only the brief accounts of Dutch ancestry promulgated by the Wyckoff Association of America.

must then officially and publicly disavow the two works so frequently cited on internet as data sources: *Old World Progenitors of the Wyckoff Family*, and the introduction to the 1950 *Wyckoff Family in America*. It is especially urgent that the opening page of the current CD version of the Wyckoff genealogy be revised, particularly the listing of Claes Cornelisz van Shouw and Margaret Van der Goes as the parents of Pieter Claessen Wyckoff. Only after such performative acts will the Wyckoff Association earn the trust of both amateur and professional genealogists. If a family association is known to dispense false information, all trust is lost. No one wants to pay a membership fee for false information.

Thirdly, the Wyckoff and other family associations, along with professional genealogists, must tap into the gigantic and growing market for genealogy enterprise. There are numerous websites devoted just to supplying the meanings of surnames. Most all genealogy websites have at least a section on the meaning of the surname. People really do want to know the etymology of their name. Unfortunately, much of the available information is blatantly false. The word must get out to the millions of amateurs that better information is available. Amateurs could play a role in refuting falsehoods, but first they must have reliable sources that can be cited.

Conventional mailings to surname lists that could be compiled from WhitePages should not be overlooked. There is great potential for increasing memberships. A very small percentage of the people on such surname lists actually belong to a responsible family association. Family associations can print and promote reliable sources, preferably on their official websites, but only after they have publicly purged remnants of past misinformation. Annual memberships to family associations should be reasonably priced to compete with genealogy dotcoms. Volunteer historians and genealogists should be actively solicited and rewarded whenever possible. As part of the fee for membership, members should be offered a significant discount on a personal DNA profile. A reliable DNA testing laboratory should be commissioned to test all current and potential members of the Wyckoff Association of America who request it. DNA testing will be as common as fingerprints in the future. Family associations could be leading the application to genealogy.

To dismiss the Frisian origin of Pieter Claessen as controversial, as has been done by members of the Wyckoff Association in the past, only resuscitates the ghost of Gustave Anjou and lends credence to mendacity. The whole truth may never be known, but it would be a propitious act if the Wyckoff Association of America could defeat inertia by reassuring the descendants of Pieter Claessen that the genealogical account has finally emerged from the maze of dead-end alleys and is now headed in the right direction. Members of the Wyckoff House Foundation are to be congratulated for the years of effort it took to save the Wyckoff homestead in Brooklyn. Hopefully, an old Dutch American barn can be reconstructed on site to house a real living museum, with a team of Frisian horses to pull a carriage, and a Holstein-Frisian cow that school children can witness being milked by hand.

The Wyckoff family of America can still take pride in their Dutch heritage directly through the mother of Grietje van Ness, but the Frisian heritage can no longer be denied. When lineages were never recorded and are otherwise unavailable for genealogy, there need be no despair. We can still learn and enjoy much about the history, archaeology, genetics, and linguistics of the communities from which our ancestors emigrated to America. From our contemporary nationalistic perspective, we tend to overemphasize the contributions of one culture over another when our origins were actually multicultural from the beginning. (Even though the explorer Henry Hudson sailed for Holland, he was not Dutch, but English). The Dutch American cultural heritage deserves to be celebrated especially for encouraging the usage of other languages, its tolerance of other cultures, and for its explicit solicitations for settlers from many countries.

Epilogue

Sadly, this treatise is not being published as a special issue of the Wyckoff family *Bulletin*. In 2012, I proposed that my first draft of this work be utilized by the Association to re-launch the publication of the *Bulletin* and a newsletter, either hard copy or online, to satisfy the demand of Wyckoff descendants in America for good up-to-date information on genealogy and family history. Indeed, it was a large part of my motivation to divert time and effort away from my academic pursuits. I offered to donate any remuneration that the sale of a special *Bulletin* might bring to the Wyckoff country store. I hoped that this article would stimulate interaction and active participation of Association members, and that it would be facilitated by Association leadership, but it was not to be. There appears to be little interest in reviving the family *Bulletin*. I see no evidence of fund raising proposals or long-term strategic planning. I see no effort to market membership in the Association to a very large pool of Wyckoff descendants across America and in Germany. I have still not been informed how widely my draft was disseminated and my proposal discussed by the leadership. I am aware that at least three letters were sent to the President of the Wyckoff House Foundation and Association urging publication. Two of the three genealogists are direct descendants of Pieter Claessen; none received the courtesy of a reply. Without the support of Association leadership in providing genealogical and historical services, I fear the dwindling membership will only continue to decline.

236. CANAL WITH A LARGE BOAT
1650   *two states*

Figure 11. Rembrandt etching of boat docked at a wharf such as one might have observed at The Wykhof in the early 17th century and before. *The Complete Etchings of Rembrandt*, edited by Bruce and Seena Harris. Crown Publishers, 1970.